THE INCOMPLETE DANGLER

MERVYN LINFORD

THE LITTORAL PRESS

First Published in 2004

The Littoral Press
38 Barringtons, 10 Sutton Road,
Southend-on-Sea, Essex. SS2 5NA
United Kingdom

© Mervyn Linford 2004

The right of Mervyn Linford to be identified as author
Of this work has been asserted by him under
The Copyright Designs and Patents Act 1988

British Library Cataloguing-in-Publication Data
A catalogue record of this book is available from
The British Library

ISBN 0-9541844-3-2

Photographs: Clare Harvey

Printed by 4Edge Ltd, Hockley, Essex.

CONTENTS

1 Beginnings

2 Further Afield

3 Chelmer Memories

4 Foreign Waters

5 Seaweed – Sand – and Saltwater

6 Dover and Deal

7 Paglesham Pie – Blackwater Bass

8 Winged Horse Angling Club

9 New Friends – Same Waters

10 Billericay and District Angling Club

11 The Lion at Thurne

12 Lands End to John o'Groats

13 Mopeds and Maggots

14 Belaugh to Beccles

15 'Last Lines'

PROLOGUE

ALL SAINTS (ULTING – RIVER CHELMER)

There is a church beside the river -
An ancient place of stone and flint – living
The lessons of an age that's passing. Sermons
Are different now – the diving tern

Dips to the icon of its sacred self –
Shatters the instant with a dream that's delving.

The Gospel is the cadence of a warbler –
A wash of notes – that daily – as they daub
Leave the mind a mural made of sound.
Moorhens pierce the passion of their vows –

Where light reflects the image of a spire
And captures clouds. The alders – are a choir –

A whispered susurration of the air
Where leaves are tongues of language –like a prayer –
And preaching is the purpose of the sun.
The celebrant – is sentience – and summer

As thoughts of something other touch the ear
And visions are the vespers of revering.

Ecclesiastic order here divines
The depths that drown with miracles of fish –
The moment – in itself – is bread and wine
Beyond the realms – of reverence – and wishes.

CHAPTER ONE

BEGINNINGS

I was hatched – as is appropriate to all good angling stories – in Fleet in Hampshire in June 1946. Having had a life-long love of the countryside – lakes and rivers especially – I'd like to think that being born in rural parts authenticates my credentials as a bone fide bucolic. Unfortunately, the truth is I was only born in Fleet because of The Second World War. My parents and their parents all originated in such illustrious places as Custom House, Canning Town and Silvertown in the East End of London, and my mother only moved into the wilds of Hampshire because of the Blitz and other sundry wartime inconveniences. So genetically and spiritually my real home was made up of slums, bombsites, docks, belching smokestacks, jellied eels – fishy at least – pie and mash, sarsaparilla and Rathbone Street Market! Nevertheless, The Laurels, 64 Westover Road, Fleet, Hampshire, was to be - and still is - my one and only claim to genuine rusticity. I left Fleet to return to the prefabs and the city when I was only three years old, so my memories of the place are vague and somewhat sketchy to say the least. I remember a small black and white dog, a bridge, what subsequently turned out to be watercress beds, and somewhat surrealistically – goldfish! Those subaqueous seams of rippling scales and muscle obviously swam deep into my developing subconscious and primed my life-long love of all finned and pharyngeal denizens of the shallows and the depths. London and the Thames was a different kettle of conundrums altogether. In those delightful days of pestilence and pollution the average flounder wouldn't be seen dead – and I use the word advisedly – without a Mickey Mouse gas mask and a de-contamination suit! The river was as thick as chocolate after rain and yellow and sulphurous the rest of the time. The only shoal-fish known to inhabit that onetime rancid watercourse were the ubiquitous brown-scaled Richard the slippery Thirds!!! Angling would have to wait until I partook of my second pseudo-bucolic experience. My father was given the option of exchanging his prefab for a house in West Ham Borough or moving to Basildon New Town. Fortunately, for the aspiring angler, he chose the latter. Basildon in those days consisted of just two estates: Whitmore Way to the northwest and Barstable to the south, where I was bound to reside. Other than those two enclaves of incipient urbanism - Laindon in the west, Wickford to the north, and Pitsea, the creeks, fleets, marshes and the Thames Delta to the south - all was fields, farms, smallholdings, orchards, elms and thorn thickets – a paradise indeed! By this time - 1951 - I was five years old and already infused with the pioneering spirit. In those prepubescent times - devoid it seems of perverts and paedophilia - I was allowed the privilege of a completely free rein and spent many a happy hour wandering around the countryside on my own. There were ponds – mostly it's said, bomb craters that were bone dry in August but full to the brim with water, frogs, toads, newts and sticklebacks in spring – and ditches by the dozen just waiting in the sparkling shafts of sunlight for the withy and the ever eager angle! I cut my piscatorial teeth on those sticklebacks. The males were darting gems in those diminutive waters: silver and black, ruby throated, and with eyes like sapphires. All you needed by way of equipment and bait was a bent pin, string and a worm. Sometimes they fell off the hook before you got them to the waiting jar, and this early experience of watery disappointment was etched deep into my developing circuitry and still exhibits itself in its full electrifying force whenever my pole-rig and a double figure carp part company. Such is life! Have you ever really looked at sticklebacks in a jar? The curvature of the glass plays strange optical tricks and those tiny, jewel-like, delicate fish, can sometimes take on a weight and a demeanour of alarming proportions. I think that this may be where the propensity for adding extra pounds and ounces to one's diminutive catch had its origination – well that's my story and I'm sticking to it hook, line and bloody sinker!!! Newts are not exactly fish, I'll give you that, but they are wet, spend a lot of time under water, and are ideal for honing one's infantile angling skills. Worms and wool were the ideal tackle, but whether the quarry appreciated being held by the tail after capture and being swung round above one's head, is something a helicopter pilot alone could tell you! Mind you, a dizzy newt corkscrewing its way back to the bottom of a ditch with out the aid of alcohol is a sight to gladden the eye of any recovering dipsomaniac! The seeds of fishing were not just sown by the whispering whiteness's of the freshwater crowsfoot but also by the salted breath of sea lavender, purslane and thrift. The marshes, fleets, creeks and saltings of the Thames Delta were my oyster – to coin a serendipitous phrase!

Such evocative names spring to mind as: Timberman's Creek, Vange Creek, Pitsea Hall Island, Benfleet Creek, Fobbing Horse and Holehaven Creek, to name but a few – What inspired nomenclature! Although still relatively young and unable to afford the required tackle, that didn't stop me from watching the older boys and the men practicing their piscatorial arts in the tideways of that enchanted corner of East Saxonia – or Essex to the uninitiated! Flounders, which for some reason start off round and end up flat, were plentiful. Fish of two pounds or more were not uncommon and if fished for with light tackle – especially freshwater float gear – put up a spectacular fight. School bass were ledgered or spun for and their spinning silver scales captured the sunlight like a thousand mirrors. Eels were a marshland speciality. I'm told – by an Anorak of my acquaintance – that most of the eels we catch are only up to two years old as after that time they return to the Sargasso sea from whence they came in order to spawn – or whatever eels do by the way of sex! The monsters that are caught – as thick as your arm and as slippery as a car salesman – are, I'm reliably informed, sterile, and therefore have no urge to return to their Caribbean roots. These watery representations of the eunuch and the virgin grow to inordinate lengths to avoid sex – and being caught by worm dangling voyeurs. But caught they were by the stewed and jellied bucket full. I've seen grown men turn to whimpering tearful wrecks as they wrestled with the slimy leviathans in the sinuous and constricting marshland grasses – formidable adversaries indeed! When I think of just how often we swam in those salt laden waterways I'm surprised that we weren't torn limb from limb by those carnivorous, piranha-like, monsters of the deep – not to mention the possibility of their smaller cousins entering every available bodily orifice – it doesn't bear thinking about, does it? As Jack Hargreaves once so wisely said, fishing is not just about fish, it's also about 'the angler's other eye'. Those marshes and tidal flats were a haven for wildlife - waders and wildfowl especially. Redshank tweked, shelduck laughed eerily, curlew called their solitary calls, and oystercatchers bleeped from their sub tropical, coral coloured bills. It was a prelapsarian wonderland. Peewits and herons rose on angelic wings, godwits and teal and widgeon were cherubim and seraphim to my newly religious eyes, and all the principles and powers of the heavenly hierarchy floated to earth in the name of dunlin and turnstone and knot. It was not just sea birds that coloured the eye with their exotic plumage but passerines and raptors preened and perambulated throughout the thorn thickets and the reed-margined fleets. Magpies chattered in the sloe and hawthorn, bearded reedlings flitted through the whispering reeds, linnets and redpolls undulated in flight, warblers warbled, and whitethroats rattled their love songs in the scrub. Skylarks rose to infinity, or almost, a pencil point, a full stop to their own song. Sparrow hawks soared and kestrels hovered, voles and shrews and small birds cowered in the predatory grasses, foxes stalked, and rabbits and hares twitched and quivered on the edge of cover. Pitsea Fleet was an especially interesting area of brackish water. Apart from the ubiquitous eels, before it was inundated by the sea in the Great Tide of 1953 it was home to some particularly stupendous rudd. I sat and watched as they rippled the summer surface of the fleet to such a concentric effect that you would think you were witnessing a shower of rain falling from a blue and cloudless August sky. Some of the locals freelined floating crust or used a bubble float to tempt those animate jewels. The golden sides and red resplendent fins of the rudd are a joy to behold – once seen, and especially handled, never to be forgotten. Some of those glorious creatures of God's creation reached the specimen size of two pounds or more and to see the sun-shot crystal spray as they were played across the surface to the waiting net, was as if to see the sun itself explode and shatter into red and golden fire. My first real fishing was practiced at a diminutive local fishery, known less than originally, as the Willow Pond. It was an oasis of willows and water crowsfoot deep amongst the surrounding scrub and elm-lined farmland to the north of Pitsea. One of the willows was of the old, gnarled variety, with broken limbs and trailing silvery leaves and branches. Sometimes in the summer the seed floss would blow on the warming breeze and settle on the water's surface like an unseasonable snowfall. Dragonflies – known locally as the Devil's darning needles – stitched and unstitched the humid air, hovered like kestrels, then shot off at lightning speed in search of prey. Water boatmen - boated, pond skaters - skated, great diving beetles dived and surfaced in silver bubbles, frogs croaked and damselflies danced on their delicate blue and green metallic wings. If the marshes were prelapsarian then this was Paradise indeed. Ambrosia was bread and sugar sandwiches, nectar, ginger beer or Adam's Ale for the less than fortunate, and the golden cups of floating lilies drank in the shafted honey of the omniscient and omnipresent sunlight. Here there were swimming grass snakes, and tribes of primitive boys and adolescents splashed about in the frenetic margins to rid the waters of imaginary pythons and anacondas. Mute swans - as white and wild as a dream of the Arctic – whispered their muted expletives as we disturbed their summer reveries, and blackbirds chinked their high-pitched, full-throated glasses, as they toasted us with the urgency of their alarm calls. Whenever silence ensued thoughts of crucian carp and fishing became of paramount importance. Swims were few and lily-padded so invariably when it came allocating the prime positions the biggest boys – as always in this cruel life of ours – caught the biggest fish. Not that the fish were that big in all honesty. The pond must have been knee deep in stunted crucian carp ranging from tiddlers to what we at that time considered specimens of around six inches at the most! But did it matter? Did it hell! Tackle was still somewhat primitive to say the least: a willow switch sufficed as a rod, 16 hooks, once purchased, were prized and cared for as if they were part of the Gold Standard. Floats were handmade from cork and matchsticks and painted and varnished with all the skill, love, and inspiration attributed to Renaissance painters and the illuminators of ecclesiastical manuscripts. This was serious stuff. Mr. Crabtree had been read in rapt and religious silence, Bernard Venables absorbed and assimilated, and baits prepared with secret essences such as custard powder and pilchard oil – the relating of which still smacks of the utmost in angling heresy! In the heat of the long, hot, summer days, bites were few and far between, but when the shadows lengthened and the swifts and swallows lifted into the cool benighted skies and the pipistrelle bats tickled the water's surface with their prehistoric wings, the crucians started to feed. And what fish they were! If you think that a willow switch is not the perfect rod for crucians; then try one for yourself. They had the perfect all through action for our young and inexperienced hands, anything stiffer and we'd have probably bumped off more fish than we caught. As it was we caught plenty of the thick-muscled, aureate-scaled, mini leviathans. Ounce for ounce I think they shake, circle, dive and fight as hard and as long as any fish in British waters – sea fish, silvers or otherwise. These days I manage to catch crucians of well over two pounds on occasions, and beautiful fish they are too, but nothing can compare with those early days of improvised tackle and limited resources. In my childish imagination they were more valuable that all the treasure plundered from the Spanish Main. To hold one in my young hands, to feel all the pent up power in their glint and golden muscles, was the closest I had been to heaven on earth, and the memory of fishing for crucian in those early days is still associated in my mind with the spirit guardians of the Willow Pond, and the primal Gods of pectorals and pure Platonic form!

CHAPTER TWO

FURTHER AFIELD

You'd think what with having Hampshire as my birthright and having visions of goldfish and watercress at an early age, that rivers like the Itchen and the Test would be well and truly in my blood. Not a bit of it! Up to my early teens lakes and ponds – apart from the creeks and the sea – were my sole outlet for piscatorial diversions. The nearest river – or more accurately, the Chelmer/Blackwater Navigation – was some twenty miles distant and not conducive to spindly legs, inordinate amounts of fishing tackle, and a clapped-out, antiquated, velocipede! Chub and dace would have to wait until motorized transport became available. For the time being all of my fishing would have to be done within easy peddling range. Woody's is the first lake that springs immediately to mind. It was situated behind the Bull Inn and Corringham's equally ancient village church, surrounded by elms and the flappable purple sheen of garrulous rooks. It was an old gravel working that had matured over the years into a natural looking tree-lined fishery. The margins had the occasional sporadic swathes of reeds and rushes, and there were one or two patches of lily-pads – which in early summer held golden goblets in their green uplifting palms. On the western side of the lake there were a few caravans owned by Woody himself, a bungalow and a very respectable tackle shop. We fished for crucian, tench, bream, roach, rudd and perch. There were common carp in the lake but in those days they were considered so wary and cunning that it would be a waste of valuable fishing time trying to catch them. Nowadays it seems that carp are so ravenous and competitive on a diet of 'boilies' and 'fish pellets' that those with expensive polarized glasses swear that they've seen double figure carp queuing up to ascend the dangled lengths of any available monofilament!!! How times change. Poor old Dick Walker must be turning in his sparsely populated heavenly thermocline! He is dead, isn't he? I hope so – if you see what I mean. No, Woody's was no Redmire Pool, but to the prepubescent danglers of worms and bread flake it was more than adequate. I – as the title of this book indicates – was very rarely in the frame, but I did catch the occasional decent fish which was more than enough to keep me happy. One of my friends I nicknamed Gibbo the Tench. He could have caught the little tincas down a drain – I'm sure of it. The red-eyed doctor fish were his speciality. Most of the tackle I fished with had been begged, borrowed, or stolen, but he had an Allcock's Gloria and a spanking, brand new, aluminium centre-pin reel. He fished light, either laying-on or using the lift method with worm or bread for bait, and invariably stole the honours from June to September. To me the various species of fish are a bit like the seasons – whichever one I'm in, or whatever type of fish I'm catching – is for that particular moment my special favourite. I'm not fickle; I'm eclectic – so there! One of the regulars at the waterside was an Irishman known predictably as Paddy Cane. Cane by name cane by nature - his wooden tackle was that old that we all assumed that he had purchased it from Noah himself! But this particular Bernard o Venables was always one hook, line, and sinker, ahead of the sniggering Anglo Saxons. The man had more blarney than a bookmaker and had the Celtic effrontery to name the species of fish he was about to catch before he'd even had a nibble! What was worse he always used the same bait – the 'worum' and nothing but the 'worum'. I don't know whether or not he had a direct link to the patron saint of fishermen 'he's self', but being a devout Catholic I suspected that St Peter was definitely on his side. Whatever, if he said he was going to catch a bream next, then 'be'geebers' he caught one! "It 'ul be a tench," he would say, and it was. "I tink I'll be having a perch," and a perch he definitely had. It was infuriating, but give the man his due; he knew the water like the back of his hand and knew exactly what he was doing. If I'd have paid more attention to his tackle and his methods perhaps I'd have become a 'Complete Angler' far sooner than later instead of vainly trying to get beyond the veil in my dreams and my meditations for a one to one with old Izaak himself!!! Another thing I experience at Woody's for the first time – was night fishing. For a group of eager youngsters a tent by the rushes with the moonlight glittering on the water was the epitome of excitement and adventure. Not all was calm and tranquil though – not by a long chalk. To the south of the lake, across a couple of miles of fleets and marshes, lay the Thames Haven Oil refineries. At the time one of the scariest programmes ever to have been broadcast on television – before or since I might add as I twitch and tremble into hair-raising recollections – was 'The Quatermass Experiment'. Much of the spine-chilling series was shot at those very refineries. In one particular episode an unfortunate individual was thrown into one of the large spherical tanks containing a particularly corrosive liquid. For the 1950's the special effects were pretty good. As he sunk into the viscous liquid you could see the flesh peeling off of his bones and although things were black and white in those days you could imagine his blood leaching and bubbling in the acidic environs! On one of our night fishing escapades we dared ourselves to walk the perimeter of the lake in near pitch darkness. As we passed a hedge overlooking the eerie, flickering glow of the distant refineries, an apparition rose like Lazarus from the dead and lunged at us through the moon-silvered foliage. "Eff off you frigging bastards," he expleted, with a face as contorted and corrosive as the corpse in the tank of aforementioned acid, "can't a man get any frigging sleep round 'ere?" He was probably just a gentleman of the road utilizing God's own grass-lined and leafy green four-poster, but at that particular moment such rational thoughts were far from our irrational minds! Traction was difficult on the dew dampened greensward but suffice it to say we managed to put a considerable distance between ourselves and that festering visage of the wildwoods! Have you ever run around in ever decreasing circles not knowing quite what to do and why, with your heart pounding away like a pile-driver in overdrive? Well I have and I can assure you getting the adrenaline back into its ductless glands makes camels and the eyes of needles seem like a piece of piss! We were terrified, but even under the lunar influence, sanity eventually returned and we realized that the man was only trying to get a kip, and that 'things that go bump in the night' are usually bream rolling and rollocking on the surface of the moon-gladed waters. Mind you, back in the tent, the hooting of owls and the barking of foxes did little to reassure us or soothe our shattered nerves. Still, such was Woody's and the ways of our wayward youth. Now that I'm older I much prefer the nocturne to the symphony of sunlight and the sounds of nature in the still and early hours are as soothing to me as the slime on the glistening silhouette of a midnight tench!

Bata's was another small lake that we frequented. It was situated about half way between Corringham and Fobbing. Truth be known we shouldn't have been frequenting it at all - mainly because it was strictly private! But such are the recalcitrant ways of adolescence. Is it any different nowadays? I doubt it. A one pound roach on day ticket water is something special – is it not? But an illegal one pound roach is something to die for! There's not a Peterman in the world that has not experienced the same illicit joys as we did when cracking the safe of that prohibited lake. Stealth was the watchword. We assembled our tackle in the field beyond the fishery, baited up, and crept like Apaches through the surrounding hedges and undergrowth. Not a twig was snapped as we soft-footed our way towards the unsuspecting quarry. The lake was hardly ever fished and as a consequence of this fact the fish were both unwary and ravenous. Rudd like gold bars came thrashing to the nets to be admired and assayed. Big, pink-bellied roach – smelling like the crux of all that's rivery – soiled our tainted hands with illegal silver, and perch with felonious stripes pumped and plunged to the abysmal depths of our depraved piscatorial imaginations. We were never caught red-handed in the act of poaching. The lake was surrounded by trees and hedges and the owner's house was hidden from most of the bays and inlets by the mass of summer foliage. The only places I catch fish as easily and frequently as I did in Bata's in those days is on the ubiquitous commercials – and what's more I have to pay handsomely for the privilege! Free fishing; free legal fishing; dream on my maggot-riddled friends – dream on!

Stanford Warren, now there's a name where memories abound. Owned by The Shell Mex Angling Club and open to day tickets, it was – and still is – a large complex of lakes, islands and promontories, connected by deep channels, bridges and wooden walkways. To the west lies Mucking church and in-between a nature reserve supporting the largest area of phragmites reeds in Essex. Nowadays the reserve is famous for its population of bearded reedlings, water voles protected from the deprivations of mink and other carnivorous escapees, lizards and adders. I often walk the dogs along a pathway that cuts straight through the centre of the reed beds. Lining the pathway there are sloe and hawthorn and wild plum. The reeds on either side are constantly alive with the rasp and rattle of sedge and reed warblers. Every spring I get out my field guide and try to determine which are which. One species it's said sing – if that's the right word – both louder and slower than the other. But do you think I can remember which is which? Not a chance. My ears are attuned whilst I'm there with the field guide in my hand to refer to, but no sooner do I get home and put the book back on the shelf than I immediately forget which is which and have to go through the same infuriating procedure every time I visit the reserve. I have the same trouble with coots and moorhens. Telling them apart in open water is no problem at all – I might not be an Anorak, but I'm not a complete wally – an 'incomplete' one maybe! No, it's when they're skulking in the reeds that the difficulty arises. When I see one in the flesh – or the feather if you see what I mean – simultaneously with its call, then I'm convinced I'll remember one from the other. But as soon as they disappear back into the reeds – hark! Is that a coot or is that a moorhen? Will I ever know for sure – I doubt it. But never mind, happiness is ignorance, or so some dim witted pseudo philosopher was prone to spout reassuringly at the mentally challenged! I even have trouble with old Philomel. Is it a song thrush whose been taking singing lessons or is it the one-time resident of Berkley Square? Not all is lost. I bought myself a tape of birdsongs a number of years ago and although I still have a certain amount of difficulty identifying a number of my avian friends, I have most of the common birds and even some of the rarer species well and truly sorted. Perhaps I'll get my I-Spy Badge after all – or is it I-Hear? I digress; let's get back to the past and the willowy, fish-concentric waters of Stanford Warren. One of my first really successful tench sessions took place on the smallest lake in the complex – known appropriately as the 'child's pond'. I cycled down with my friend Pancho before dawn on one warm and starlit night in late June. We'd gone all out this time; we'd read all the pertinent literature on the subject, mixed a heap of breadcrumb with chopped worms and ox blood, and sharpened our hooks as well as our intellects. As we tackled up in the crepuscular light, swarms of bats were changing shifts with equally abundant swifts and swallows. Fish were jumping everywhere and the slap of their sides on the silky water was echoed by the plop and splash of our descending groundbait. I was fishing with a ten foot split cane rod, four pound line; a six inch quill float and a number twelve eyed hook tied directly to the monofilament. Fishing slightly over depth in the still unruffled waters as the first rays of breaking sunlight illuminated the trees on the far bank, my float bobbed a couple of times then sailed away under the water at an angle of about 45 degrees. It was my first real tench; three muscular pounds of olive-sided obstinacy requiring side-strain, time, and nerves of tempered steel. Eventually after a long and powerful fight it came to the net thrashing in the crystal spray like a demented denizen of Neptune's watery domain. We both caught a net-full of tench ranging between one and three pounds in weight and my love of the doctor fish doubled and trebled and quadrupled with every bite. There were apocryphal stories of enormous eels being caught in the deep channels that connected some of the many lakes in the complex. Another friend – Dennis – decided to go for bust and fish for them exclusively. On one occasion I joined him for a night-fishing session. Our tackle was heavy; strong, eight foot, solid fiberglass boat rods, 15lb line, a running ledger and a wire trace with a number 6 hook. To the aforementioned tackle we lip-hooked sprats, lobbed them out into the deepest water and awaited results. I don't know about you but the combination of darkness, deep water, dead bait, and the thought of the ravenous maws of marauding leviathans does nothing to instill in me a sense of peace and perfect tranquility. In fact on that particular occasion foreboding would have been the understatement of all understatements! I was shitting myself. Fortunately, being as already verified, the most 'incomplete' of all 'incomplete danglers', I didn't have a bite all night. But Dennis did – oh yes he did!!! As strong as his rod was it curved as though he'd struck into a veritable conger. Eels pump and plunge as only eels no how, but slowly and surely the strength of the tackle overcame the slippery, writhing weight, of that wriggling giant from the depths of some serpent-spitting hell. The eel was some five pounds in weight and to watch Dennis grapple with the ferocious coiling beast – from a safe distance I hasten to add – was to a young teenager with a vivid imagination terrifying in the extreme. Nowadays I see eels in a different light altogether. I've grown quite found of them really – apart from the jellied and stewed variety that is – and see them as no more or less than another example of God's fish-fingered creativeness. Tubby Issacs can say what he likes, but I for one have given up eating the delightful creatures. It's bad enough being sterile without being bumped on the head with a 'priest', cut up into manageable pieces and boiled in one's own fat! No, as far as I'm concerned, eels and my good self are all brothers and sisters under the skin; no more or less than different expressions of God's diverse and infinite thought processes. If they can't go home to the far Sargasso Sea and mingle with their relatives then I'm more than happy to see them take up permanent residence in these Sceptred Isles surrounded by a silver sea – after all, I'm no xenophobe – am I?

In the vicinity of Pound Lane in North Benfleet there was another local pond known as Jackson's. This particular pond sat – if ponds can be said to sit that is – on top of a hill between All Saints Church and the eponymous farmstead itself. As can well be imagined; in the days before the ravages of Dutch elm disease the pond exhibited itself as something of a rare and rustic idyll to our city oriented eyes. Geese honked and ducks dabbled. Cows mooed and sheep bleated and did unspeakable things with their own diminutive droppings! Another friend of mine in those far off dreamy days was Dave Parks. He was a completely different kettle of fish – to use the appropriate terminology – from all the other prepubescents I was acquainted with. It has to be said that he was rather forward for his age – he did eventually put his milt in the wrong place and fertilized a spawn heavy girl of just fifteen years of age. I have subsequently heard that they got married when they reached the legal definition of consenting adults and went on to produce a ravening shoal of screaming tiddlers!!! Or human fry if you wish to be pedantic. I digress yet again. This lothario of the lakeside would insist on bringing his latest girlfriend – or catch as he preferred to say piscatorially – on our supposedly all male fishing trips. Crucian carp and roach are one thing but a hand full of sprats caught from the corner of one's eye as one is dutifully trying to angle the dangle is another. This could be the very reason why I still associate fish with naked women!!! It has the social advantage of keeping my sybaritic therapist in the luxury to which she has become so regally accustomed, and no doubt the profit orientated drug companies are more than happy to keep supplying me with more than my fair share of 'Largactyl' – chlorpromazine to the mentally adept or insane amongst you. But for me accusations of bestiality are very hurtful. Okay, I love fish, but I can assure you that it's purely a platonic relationship. Is it my fault that my young and somewhat impressionable mind was to be irrevocably confused by the incongruous juxtapositioning of crucian carp and golden pubic hair – is it, I ask you? I can't count the times that I've taken a girl home from the pub and groundbaited the bed before I realized that she wasn't a mermaid! If anyone knows of a cure for this psychological disorder please write it on a PVA bag and send it to the publisher's address – I would be extremely grateful, and perhaps fish might even stop winking at me in the depths of my deep subconscious dreams! Well, I think that that's more than enough of ponds and puberty for the moment. It's time to leave the lakes and ponds of Southeast Essex and to move off far into the rural hinterland of the county and to wet a line or two in the slow, reflective, waters of The Chelmer/Blackwater Navigation. See you on the bank – tight lines!

CHAPTER THREE

CHELMER MEMORIES

The Chelmer/Blackwater Navigation was opened for business in 1796. The two rivers which gave it its name both started within a mile or so of each other on the hills in the north western corner of Essex. From there both rivers headed of in opposite directions before circling round and joining together again at Beeleigh weir just to the west of Maldon. At one end the navigation terminated in Chelmsford at a location known as Springfield Basin. In the original plans for the canal the other end was supposed to be in Maldon itself but due to local opposition a cut – known as The Long Pond – was eventually excavated between Beeleigh and Heybridge. Heybridge basin – as it became known – was an ideal site because the new sea lock opened out into Collier's Reach on the tidal River Blackwater where there was a depth of water capable of accommodating larger vessels than would have otherwise been the case. The main trade was in coal, lime, chalk, timber and coke, and was carried on prosperously until superceded by the newly-built railways in the 1840's. The last trading vessels on the navigation were motorized timber barges operated by Brown & Sons of Chelmsford and these continued to ply their trade right up until 1972! In 1948 after a period of particularly heavy winter rain the canals walls were breached at Beeliegh and for a time it was thought that that would be the final nail in the coffin of the once prosperous navigation. Fortunately for anglers and boating enthusiasts some quick thinking soul thought of scuppering a couple of barges and building the retaining walls around and over them. This action ultimately saved the canal which is now a much loved haven for fishermen, pleasure boating types and wildlife.

I personally have fished – what I've always know as the River Chelmer – since the late 1950's. It was an exceptionally prolific river fish-wise and being as for most of its length it was completely isolated from the more industrialized parts of Essex as it meandered through its valley surrounded by low hills, woods and farmland, it was also aesthetically very pleasing as well. Sadly, during the late 60's and 70's it suffered a number of major setbacks. Insecticides and herbicides of a particularly virulent nature decimated the area's wildlife and severely depleted the fish stocks. The use of artificial fertilizers added to the weed growth in the river and what with this and increased water abstraction things were beginning to look very bleak indeed! As if all of this wasn't enough the waterway was then struck by a disease which was a disaster for its perch stocks – a disaster of national proportions – and finally to add insult to injury Dutch elm disease did its best to turn some of the riverside copses into skeletal, leafless, graveyards. I can remember in the mid 60's seeing such birds as peregrine falcons by day and nightjars and nightingales at dusk. Partridge – both red-legged and English – were plentiful, along with pheasants of differing varieties. Insecticides in the food chain put pay to the peregrines, nightjars and nightingales, and the agricultural rush for ever-increasing profits meant that the farmers started ploughing right up to the field edges, leaving no headlands. In an intensively farmed landscape headlands are extremely important. Game bird chicks are scientifically known as 'precocious'. This means that when they are hatched they immediately start feeding for themselves and need little or no assistance from their parents. The headlands provided the ideal habitat for wild flowers and these in turn attracted an enormous variety of insects. Fortunately, in recent years farmers have begun to realize the necessity of a more balanced approach to agriculture and the headlands have returned along with the missing pheasants and partridges! Is there hope for the future? I for one, certainly hope so!!!

The River Chelmer has numerous locks, mill-pools, weirs and small tributaries along its entire length and as far as features for angling are concerned you couldn't wish for a more salubrious environment. Despite the ravages of Dutch elm disease all is not lost. Farmers and willow merchants work in partnership to grow and process the exceptionally fast growing cricket bat willow and these delicate and graceful trees line the banks and cast their feathery reflections into the receptive waters. Alders are also prevalent and their overhanging leaves and boughs shelter some enormous chub. Apart from willows and alders there are small copses and spinneys all along the river harbouring a variety of other tree species such as: poplar, ash, lime, oak, hawthorn and sloe. This area of

Essex is well known for its sand and gravel deposits and as a result apart from the river itself there are plenty of pits available to the angler as well. When I was a teenager in the early 60's many of these were still working pits but now in 2004 most of them have matured wonderfully and serve to augment the natural beauty of the surrounding countryside. Although during the construction of the navigation much of the river was deepened, straightened, and widened, there are still many places were it follows the course of the original River Chelmer and as a consequence looks far more natural than many of the other canals that criss-cross the English landscape. Well, hopefully that describes something of the paradise I was about to enter into in the late 1950's, so let's set up stall, throw in some lose feed, and cast a line or two!

I was beginning to make new friends and four of them came from one family where their angling fanatic of a father – Slasher – had given them all nicknames: Pancho, Chucky, Dibs and Turf. Turf wasn't into angling but the other three were as keen as I was. I for my untidy sins was christened – Bagwash! Four other soon to be regular fishing companions were a father and son duo: Denny and Melondrimple, the already mentioned Gibbo the Tench – God bless him – and another reject from the East End commonly known as Newmangle! To two adults had vehicles of 'sorts' – as any driver from the 50's will concur – and our normal lake fishing was soon to transmute into trotting the swim and other riverine practices. We started our excursions to the River Chelmer on June the 16th –

forget the glorious 12th, as it pales into insignificance by comparison! We were to camp over the weekend on a stretch of water between Hoe Mill and Ricketts Lock. This particular stretch had a deep slow bend, shallower runs with streamer weed, a small tributary - by a rickety wooden footbridge - that had scoured out a 15ft hole, and then more shallow water that terminated at group of riverside cottages by an iron water main that arched across the river. To get to the bank we had to walk through a copse made up mostly of giant elm trees that hung their majestic, leaf-full branches out across the sun-shot, rippling surface of the summer waterway. The dappled shade they provided cast coins of light all along the riverbank; coins far more valuable to me than any copper, silver, or gold legal tender you care to mention! We set up camp on a patch of ground close to the wooden footbridge and then made up our all-important tackle. By this time I'd managed to acquire a three piece rod of my own, which comprised of two sections of Spanish reed topped by a long, unwieldy, solid fibreglass tip; my reel if I remember correctly was of a fixed spool variety supplied by the then well known manufacturers – Intrepid. A class act - what!!! Slasher – as seniority demands – always had first pick of the swims and he invariably chose the same spot; a promontory sticking out beyond the footbridge where he fished in about six feet of water between two banks of cabbage-weed. His favourite summer baits were boiled wheat and hempseed – and he just couldn't go wrong! I copied everything he did; I'd even been known to wash and shave on the morning before I went fishing even if I didn't need to! He was a genius of the dangle, that man. Pink-bellied roach after goer roach slipped into his waiting net as he smirked knowingly in my fishless and frustrated direction. I'm convinced that some people are just born with the gift. It's as if they have some sort of direct line – excuse the pun – of communication to the totem spirits of our hunter/gatherer antecedents – I don't know! Whatever, I did eventually catch some roach, not goers admittedly, but river smelling, wonderful roach nevertheless. Gibbo the Tench was pretty hot with hempseed as well. He used one pound line, a 16 hook, and the tiniest quill float you've ever seen, shotted so as the tip barely showed above the surface of the river. Hemp bites can be very fast indeed, especially in the early part of a session, but Gibbo's reactions were more than up to the challenge. A few grains of hemp hit the water followed by the perfect cast a few seconds later. No sooner had the float cocked and settled in the water than it shot away at the speed of greased lightning! He struck firmly yet carefully at equal speed and was immediately into a fish of around the three quarters of a pound mark. The Chelmer roach were beautiful fish; some it seems were indigenous and other had been transported from the Tweed to augment the original stock. We believed that we could tell the difference between the two varieties. The Tweed being a fast game river – we felt – had given the roach a more streamline appearance than the local variety brought up on a far more sluggish lowland watercourse. Whether this was true or not I couldn't possibly tell you, but there were definitely two types of roach in the River Chelmer in those days; one form slim and extremely sinuous and the other more deep bellied and slower when hooked! Roach were not the only fish on our ever eager agendas. Dace and rudd were very prolific down the middle track and many of the deeps and features held magnificent perch. To tempt the dace and rudd we either used a bubble float or an unshotted quill to float our lines on the surface. Between the float and the hook I always used to grease my line so as the bait wouldn't sink beneath the surface. Bread flake and casters seemed to work best in those days. There were some wonderful dace in that river then, I've caught them up to 10 ounces and I'm sure that one pound plus fish were more than a possibility!!! The rudd were equally delightful. Fish of a pound were seemingly commonplace and more proficient anglers than me were capable of catching fish well over the two pound mark! On hot summer days when bottom fishing went slack and we were tired of continually casting for rudd and dace, we would try some ledgering. Ledgering with worm in the Chelmer was not always advisable, mostly because of the abundance of bootlace eels! But if you wanted a chance of catching some beautiful summer perch you had no option but to run the slippery gauntlet of our slimy friends from the Sargasso. My favourite method was to use a running ledger – cast close to the rushes on the far bank – and to stick my rod up in the rod rest as if I was beachcasting. All you needed was five pound line, a number 8 hook, and plenty of patience. But patience invariably paid off. Half pound perch were two a penny in that river in those days and fish of over a pound were far from scarce. I've waxed lyrical over many different species of fish thus far in this somewhat desultory story – but perch! What an absolutely glorious addition to the catalogue of watery existence – they are stupendous! They match their carnivorous, predatory surroundings like no other fish I know. Their striped green and yellowy flanks merge into the rushes and the cabbage weed like doom itself. If pike are the kings of the river then perch are the prince's regent! You didn't have to wait for the sort of twitchy bite you might expect from finicky bream on occasions, the rod just yanked over and the butt left the ground! And then they pumped, and then they plunged to the abysmal depths of my subaqueous imaginings. I caught many a summer perch from that river, some of which went well over a pound in weight, and are the abiding love of some of my earliest memories.

Camping over the weekend obviously meant one thing – night-fishing. I have to say that my experience of night fishing on rivers at that particular time was not exactly overwhelming. Dusk, yes - that was a different matter entirely. All I seemed to catch at night – being the 'incompletest' of all 'incomplete danglers', was eels. Slippery, slimy, crawl up your arm and cover you with snot – infuriating eels! I lost so many hooks and ended up with so many tangles that I seriously contemplated giving up fishing altogether. Well almost!!! Another thing about night-fishing that didn't entirely enamour me to the pastime in those days – apart from Slasher insisting on catching even bigger roach than he did during the day by laying-on with bread flake – was those things that go bump in the night that I mentioned earlier in this story. Across from where I was fishing – to use the term loosely – there was an enormous ash tree cradling the biggest moon you've ever seen. Owls were hooting forebodingly, water voles were splashing around my feet – or worse, perhaps rats – and the occasional large fish rattled the senses as it lifted, levitated, then crashed back into the moon-splintering water. As if all of this was not enough to scare the shit out of a mere adolescent an unseen, unsuspected, roosting heron, flew thunderously out of the ash tree in the moonlight having all the heart thumping appearance of some sort of avenging angel! I was witless! Being polite, that is! That was it, I'd had enough. Not for me the tent and moths the size of starlings; I decided to go back to the car and get my head down until first-light. I used my torch to negotiate my way through a copse that seemed to be filled with trees created by the pens and peerless imaginations of the Brothers Grimm! That reminds me – I must buy some brown underpants. The car was locked; Dibs and Chucky had managed to get there before me and had utilized all available bedroom space. There was nothing for it, I just lay down in the road next to the car and tried to sleep. At least I'd be away from the rats, the diabolical herons, and Slasher catching more roach than a Hebridian Trawlerman catches herrings!!! Apart from that I'd have two apparently human forms close by to protect me – apparently! Sleep was fitful but sufficient. I awoke somewhat bleary eyed to the sound of an impatient motor horn. During the intervening hours whilst tossing and turning in my fitful sleep I'd managed to manoeuvre myself into the middle of that admittedly very minor by-road. How the irate driver of that farm truck managed to spot me in time before flattening my carcass to the tarmac I'll never know! But fortunately for me – if not for everyone else – he did. It was bordering on first-light and breakfast was definitely of paramount importance. Breakfast, *en plein air,* at dawn by a river on a warm, calm, June day is a pleasure to be described only by the finest poets amongst us – surely? But I'll do my level best. Bacon sandwiches with great, fresh hunks of white bread, and the smell of roach on one's ravenous fingers is the epitome of epicurean delight. Blackbirds and thrushes singing their first diurnal songs, swallows and swifts skimming across the river's silks, and the sun as red and recumbent as a cache of rubies, are enough I'm sure to soften the heart of even the most stalwart of city dwellers – tell me that I'm wrong! To stand there at the river's edge looking deep into one's own reflection is to see one's spiritual self; one's eternal aspect peering back into the temporal world of dreams and illusions that we're convinced is all there is of reality – nonsense! I suspect that it is mostly anglers reading this book and therefore I'm obviously preaching to the converted, but just in case someone other than a fisherman or woman is thumbing through the pages, I feel it my bounden duty to promote this wonderful sport of ours and the environment in which it takes place to the best of my literary abilities – so there!

Summer has its joys, but so do all the other seasons of the year: 'Season of mists and mellow fruitfulness/ Close bosom friend to the conspiring sun'. Ah! The young Master Keats; he knew what he was writing about. Autumn and elderberries; autumn and the resplendent mosaic of fallen leaves carpeting the rivers misted surface – what can I say? Indian summer, St Luke's summer, it says it all – doesn't it? Does this not conjure up for you a near absolute sense of peace and tranquility – well think again! We were teenagers remember and it was nearly November the 5th! What do they say - 'Gunpowder, treason and plot'? That particular historical event was as nothing when compared with our dastardly escapades. I remember the day well. A calm, cold, overcast day in late October. Just past the overarching water main in a stretch we knew as 'Bream Bend' we decided to test our tuppenny canons! We wrapped the offending articles in balls of mud, lit the fuses, waited till they started to fizz, and then lobbed them in the river. You could see the red-suffusing glow of the explosion in the depths, closely followed by surfacing bubbles and acrid, erupting puffs of sulphurous smoke. You'll be pleased to note that we didn't manage to stun – or even kill – any passing fish, but we did something far worse – we ruined an excellent swim. Soon after we'd finished with our pyrotechnical experiments two innocent and unsuspecting adults tackled up and began to fish in the very spot we'd just bombarded with tuppenny canons!!! What can I say? The guilt still causes me sleepless nights and I pray for the soul of Guido Fawkes on a regular basis. Those poor unfortunate bastards didn't even catch a cold – let alone any of the oft-times ubiquitous tenants of 'Bream Bend'. To add insult to injury we had the audacity to go up to them and ask them if they had had any luck! Cheeky bastards – we deserved dog-ragging – and still do probably. All was not roughnecks and recalcitrance though. Autumn was probably the roachiest time of the year thereabouts and we were determined to make the most of it. On one auspicious occasion I remember sitting on the concrete apron beneath the water main with Slasher and Gibbo. The three of us – spaced equidistantly – were trotting the middle track with exceptionally light line, 18 hooks, and gentles. We couldn't go wrong. A little bit of loose feed and it was a bite a chuck. No monsters admittedly, but the shoal must have been as long as a blue whale and just as bulky! Slasher as always caught the most fish, closely followed by Gibbo - with guess who? - yours truly picking up the leftovers at the end of the swim. Mind you we had 15, 10, and 5lbs of roach respectively and in those days even the smallest weight would have been good enough to win a match or two!

Autumn – as is the way with the seasons – always turns into winter. We were stalwarts in those days, no amount of snow or frost, freezing fog or ice, rain or wind, could keep us away from our favourite pastime. I wish I could say the same today, but old bones, blood thinned and polluted by lager and pipe smoke, are not conducive to ice sharp, gale-force north easterlies or monsooning scuds shedding their drench-nasty loads out of blustering sou'westers! I do still fish in the winter – quite a lot actually – but seaweed, pine cones, and Michael Fish – now there's a name to conjure with – are my constant companions. If it's dry and over forty five degrees Fahrenheit then I'm your man, other than that it's a copy of Advanced Pole Fishing and a slug of my favourite tipple! Let's get back to more adventurous times. In one particularly severe winter –

1963 I suspect – we arrived at the river and didn't think that we'd be able to fish at all. The river was frozen solid to a depth or two feet or more! We walked across it, jumped up and down on it – foolishly perhaps – and even took to lambasting it with hammers and monkey wrenches. All to no avail – it was hopeless. That is until Slasher heard a trickle of water coming from under the bridge by the lock gates at Hoe Mill. And there it was, ten foot of open water, with room enough for the two of us to fish on the concrete apron; one each side of the bridge. It was a massacre. The river had been frozen over for weeks and this was an ideal spot for the fish to replenish their oxygen supplies. On top of that they were obviously starving! I know what you're thinking – FISH WELFARE – go on admit it!!! Well all I can say is we emptied and refilled our keepnets with prime fish more times than I'd care to remember. But in my defense I will say this: there is such a thing as quid pro quo. Like for like, an equal exchange, call it what you will. In exchange for such excellent sport we fed those poor frost-bitten fish more food than they'd probably seen for weeks, and who knows, we may have actually saved them from near certain death in one of the coldest winters on record. Well, that's my story and I'm sticking to it! I've also fished that river in some of the worst winter floods imaginable. Some would say it's pointless. What with the torrential water as slick and viscous as engine oil and having the colour and consistency of liquid chocolate, fish may well have been hard to come by – to continue with my penchant for understatement. But there were slacks by eddies on the inside of wide bends and you could always fish above the lock gates away from where the raging diluvial waterway had been diverted over weirs into back streams and on through mill ponds back into the river at the downstream side of the lock. There are always options for the less than fainthearted my friends – ALWAYS!!! Needless to say I didn't catch very much in such appalling conditions as those, but it was a day out, and after all now that I'm more of a fair weather fisherman I've got to say something to justify my piscatorial existence – haven't I? But seriously though, I have caught some very decent perch and roach in slack water on days such as I've just described – especially with girt, fat, juicy, lob worms!

Thick January frost, mist on the shivering water, and perch fishing are synonymous as far as I am concerned. Between 'Bream Bend' and Ricketts Lock there is a straight, fairly deep stretch of river that is as near as damn it featureless in winter. But it didn't seem to matter one jot. Gudgeon were easy to come by in the Chelmer. Just drop a maggot on the bottom and the float invariably sailed straight away. This was rather fortunate as my favourite method for catching perch in those days was live-baiting. On one particular frosty January day- ledgering with a paternoster set-up and lip hooking gudgeon on a number 8 hook – I caught ten perch ranging between a half and two and a half pounds. A red finned and a red letter day indeed! Once again – as with the summer perch – it was more like beachcasting than your average freshwater fishing; but none the less enjoyable for that. I said earlier on that if the pike was king then the perch were the prince's regent. Well, on a sun-shafted, silver and blue, ice-bitten, January morning they'd definitely acceded to the throne and were more than boasting their splendour in a court of reflected gold and frost. The largest of the ten is still to this day the biggest perch I've ever caught and if I never catch another one to equal or surpass it, it does not matter to me in the slightest. I catch that fish in my mind's eye every time that I see frost on the lawn in winter and the pleasure I gained from its splendid, regal company, all those many years ago will never be diminished – never! We fished in the frost and ice and we also fished in the snow. I've fished with my feet so cold and numb that I thought they belonged to someone else! I've had ice freezing in the rod rings, making it almost impossible to cast and my fingers have on occasions been so frost-embittered that I've been unable to bait the hook or roll a cigarette. But did it stop us going – did it hell! Times like those are what memories are made of. Great feathery flakes of snow shaken from the wings of winter's angels, drifting like stardust through the stark anatomy of leafless, skeletal trees; are pristine, crystal experiences, never to be forgotten. To watch a float dip through the dissolving snowflakes and to play a prime roach in the crisp and invigorating Arctic air is a pleasure never to be explained to the uninitiated. To catch a pike on a spinner in a blizzard – even a jack – is an experience the fire-hugging suburbanites of the domestic hinterland could never appreciate. A pike, thrashing in the icy waters, kicking up spray, walking on its tail, writhing in the snow laden grass beside the landing net. These are the things that even now in my more mollycoddled middle age still inspire me to break out the spinning gear and a rod with a test curve to match, and to return to the white wastes and wildernesses of the distant past, to live again the magic, the wonder, and the mystery of angling's version of love, light, and eternal youth. AMEN BROTHERS - AMEN!!!

The Willow Pond - early spring

Jackson's Pond - North Benfleet

Woody's - remember Gibbo-the-Tench?

Stanford Warren - Mervyn-the-Tench!!!

Start of 'The Long Pond' - Chelmer/Blackwater Navigation

The author - snow on Hoe Mill bridge

Ulting church - January

Hoe Mill lock

Typical Chelmer scene

Paper Mills - Little Baddow

The author - river or road - Hoe Mill?

Winter Spate - between Hoe Mill and Ricketts lock

Nowhere to fish - Ulting

Brother Dave - Chelmer bream

CHAPTER FOUR
'FOREIGN WATERS'

There was a whiff of mutiny in the air. The erstwhile happy band of anglers had taken to an inordinate amount of bickering amongst themselves. The main reason for complaint was the River Chelmer. "Why can't we try somewhere else?" The mutineers would reiterate endlessly. At first, Slasher would not be moved – he was captain and that was all there was to it! He loved the Chelmer. At less than twenty miles away from base, full of prime fish, and set in a scene of rusticated perfection, he saw no need to travel further afield. Personally, I felt much the same – though coward that I am I didn't say as much to the assembled dissenters. The Chelmer Valley was – and still is – very much my formative landscape in all senses of the words. Spiritually and materially, subjectively and objectively, temporal and eternal, conscious and subconscious, you name the abstraction – there's that nasty word again – that's where I developed my capacity for daydreaming, flights of fancy, astral travel, New Age indolence, and many another airy fairy ability so much despised in this rational world of ours! But eventually by an incessant, insidious process, of mental osmosis the mutineers won the day. Slasher finally caved in and a trip to Constable Country was organized. Why the river in question is always known as the 'Suffolk' Stour is an ever-present thorn in my piscatorial flesh. Although I've got absolutely nothing against Suffolk and words like worzel and Silly Suffolk would never pass my lips

– HONESTLY – I think that good old Essex deserves some recognition here. Without wishing to come across as pedantic, it has to be said that much of the bank pertaining to the aforementioned river is without a doubt well and truly situated in the territory of 'the white van man'! Dedham itself, centre of the tourist trade, site of some of Constable's most famous paintings, is actually an ESSEX VILLAGE. Please excuse the upper case but it makes me so angry! Who cares about Flatford Mill, the Hay Wain and Willy Lots Cottage, when there's Dedham Mill and Lock to contemplate? And what's more Alfred Munnings chose to live in Dedham and an artist with such a perfect eye for horses must have known exactly what he was doing when he chose Essex over Suffolk as his place of abode. It stands to reason – doesn't it? Well, that's enough of this inter-tribal rivalry, I'll concede that Gainsborough was a Suffolk Man – if something of a dandy – but East Bergholt aside, as far as I'm concerned Constable was an Essex man, if only by adoption. He had Essex clay on his boots. He was the reincarnation of every 'clay kicker' that ever held a palette and painted the sun-gilded majesty of cumulous clouds traversing the wide, East Saxon skies of God's own countryside. Whew! I'm glad I've got that off my chest!!! By the way, talking about Dedham brings a quaint little anecdote to mind. In the church there is a plaque on the wall commemorating a poor unfortunate woman who died as a result of swallowing a sowing implement! I bet that gave her the needle! We shouldn't laugh should we? Well, I have to say – much to my eternal shame – when I first read the plaque it certainly had me in stitches! Enough of all this nonsense – back to the fishing. In those days the mill pond car park – still situated next to a working mill rather than the luxury flats for yuppies that grace the scene nowadays – was devoid of tourists almost entirely. Those ravenous hoards of camera-swinging, snap-happy, rubber necks, debussing like a swarm of uncultured locusts, so common at this end of the twenty first century, were probably pissed and perfectly happy shagging their way through the back streets of Margate and Southend at the brewer's droop end of a works or office beano! And that's how it should have stayed as far as I'm concerned. Who needs a crowd of ice cream slurping twits gibbering and staring inanely in one's direction saying such pathetic things as " look Charlie, he's caught one?" Frigging buffoons!!! Don't they understand the seriousness of the angler's art, the watercraft, the tackle, the bait and the tactics? Apparently not, frigging morons!!! As I was saying: the car park was empty, the mill wheels were turning, and all was well with the world. By this time Slasher had bought himself a camper-van and Newmangle and I were the sole invited guests on that particular fishing expedition. We decided to fish the stone covered slope next to the mill itself. Being as it was a flour mill we'd brought a stack of boiled wheat along for bait. The water was twelve foot deep and seeing as my dilapidated rod could only manage ten feet at the most there were bound to be problems! Images of me standing on tiptoe with my rod extended skywards trying to land a fish may seem funny to you, but personally, I couldn't see the humourous side of things at all! It was then that Slasher imparted some of his secret and somewhat arcane piscatorial knowledge.

A sliding float; that's all I needed; it was as simple as that – a piece of cake you might think – well think again! Knots and my good self have always had something of an antithetical relationship. Having more thumbs than fingers is not conducive to the finer points of monofilament! I'm more of your abstract intellectual thinker than the average practical man of craftsmanship and coordination – in fact you could say that I'm somewhat cack-handed!!! After much fumbling time and frustrating effort I did manage to put in place a fairly respectable representation of the ubiquitous sliding knot – and proceeded, albeit belatedly, to angle the dangle. The roach – as always in my overactive imagination – were ravenous. We couldn't go wrong, one after another of the sweet smelling, sinuous little gems, came sliding - like quicksilver - into our waiting nets. This was angling my friends. Angling in peace-inducing isolation; 'far from the madding crowd' as good old Thomas Hardy once so fortuitously coined as a title for a far from peaceful book! It was there in that mill pool that I saw my first specimen pike. A local angler was spinning when he struck into the monster – or was it the other way round? Anyway, after a long and furious fight the beaten fish was finally netted and banked. We're now right back in the regal vicinity of the king of the river. That fish was fully twenty pounds in weight. It was as silver as a seam of misted September light, with enough sharp canines and incisors to make the average orthodontist open another bank account! The strength of that denizen of the deep was phenomenal. I helped the man unhook it, and it was so strong and powerful that to hold down its writhing, tail-flicking weight, took the combined efforts of the pair of us!!! For a time after the hook was finally removed the exhausted pike became almost lifeless. Even at my tender age I was becoming very concerned for its well-being. I needn't have worried. The revivifying qualities of pike are astonishing. We held him – or her, I've never been very good at sexing fish, or anything else for that matter, as my barren, childless existence will substantiate – gently under the water and allowed his gills to work. In no time at all his tail started to whip and he power-dove like a torpedo into the fathoming darkness of the pool. Farewell my predatory friend – farewell! By the way, going back to the Constable painting of Dedham Mill and Lock; the church is in the wrong place, poetic license I suppose. Or could it be that the locals moved it stone by stone one night while nobody was looking? Stranger things have happened! Life's a mystery my friends – an unfathomable mystery.

We didn't only fish in the mill pool at Dedham. Sometimes we'd go further downstream in the direction of Flatford to fish for chub with ledgered cheese by the roots of the overhanging alders – great fun! Not monsters, but rubbery mouthed and redolent of buried treasure – what more could you wish for? Further down – in the faster, shallower water, between two wide bends – we fished for dace and roach. Unlike the Chelmer the dace in the River Stour were quite happy to feed on the bottom, which meant that we quite often caught some very respectable mixed bags of roach and dace, along with the occasional decent perch. The dace there were some of the best, biggest, and boldest that you were ever likely to catch. I'm not sure whether or not the record dace comes from the River Stour but it was one of the finest dace rivers I've ever fished and it certainly had the potential to produce a record breaker! And fight – well it goes without saying; I can still feel the shaken reverberations of the rod travelling up my quivering arm and deep into the precincts of my electrified cranium!!! Beyond Flatford Mill – lying in Suffolk unfortunately – where we occasionally fished for roach and perch in the mill pool, there was an area with the delightful name of Judas Gap. This was where the freshwater river ended and the sea lock opened out on to tidal waters and Manningtree beyond. It was a strange place; an in-between land with rushes and reeds on one side and dykes and saltings on the other. It was nothing unusual to catch the occasional flounder in the somewhat brackish water and it was here that I caught my first mullet in one of the small tidal channels the meandered no more than fifty yards away from the river itself. When I first spotted them I was amazed, to say the least. There were roach in those tidal channels, I'd seen them before, and knew from my experiences on the tidal stretch of the Chelmer below Beeleigh Weir that this was neither exceptional nor unusual. But the mullet! Some of them were enormous! I estimate that one or two of them were around the ten pound mark. Needless to say - by the way of 'incompleteness' – they were not destined to reside in my particular landing net! But I did catch one of those soft-mouthed beauties. All I used was a free floating light line with a maggot on a 16 hook. I saw the fish take the bait – an exceptionally exciting experience as any fully-fledged fisherman – or woman – will undoubtedly tell you! A relatively clear, small tidal channel, light tackle, a pounding heart and a two pound mullet are without a doubt the recipe for some sheer, unadulterated enjoyment. It fought like the proverbial Fen Tiger in an explosion of spray and fully curved action – I was delirious!!! My first mullet, but not to be my last – NEVER! NEVER! NEVER!!!............ Apart from Dedham and Flatford we occasionally fished in a stretch of the river that meandered through water meadows surrounding the Suffolk town of Sudbury. Once when the river was in spate I fished in a chocolate-coloured side-stream and caught two fantastic roach – 1lb 12oz and 1lb 15oz - so close to the ever illusive specimen weight of 2lbs, but very special nevertheless. Another interesting thing about this particular stretch of the River Stour was that you would quite often see the locals fly fishing at dusk. I never did ask them what they were fishing for – not wishing at that tender age to appear too ignorant – but I'm sure that it wasn't wild brown trout that they were after. No, as we walked along the bank to the car park, with venus shimmering in the west and a round, recumbent moon glowing muted gold and lambently above the eastern horizon, the concentricity of innumerable circles pock marking the river's surface like the inner workings of some watery timepiece, brought rudd and the evening-Chelmer immediately to mind. That's what they were after I'm convinced of it. The evening rise and rudd are almost synonymous. I've caught them myself on dry fly since and a wonderful experience it is to see the take and strike straight in to a goer rudd as the last light peters to star-shine and the silks of shadows. There, on that lyrical note, we must leave the Suffolk Stour at least for the time being – and make our way south into the Garden of England. Kent and fishing – both sea and fresh – has always been very special to me and my angling companions and I'll start the next episode of our piscatorial journey by taking you along the willowy banks of the hop-lined and oast-housed, glorious Medway.

In the days before the Dartford Tunnel our route into Kent necessitated the use of the Tilbury Ferry. This fact made our fishing expeditions even more exciting. A sea journey – well almost! It was like going abroad. I remember one exceptionally foggy November morning in the early hours, waiting for the first ferry across the Thames. There's nothing more desolate, mournful, and plangent sounding than seabirds and sirens in the fog. It was as if you were living in an alternative reality. Curlews were the acme of isolation. Their lonely tidal calls carried in the stillness of the fog to the ends of the known world and beyond. Vessels, shrouded and dimly lit, loomed in and out of vision like chimeras crossing the Styx with Charon taking charge of the ubiquitous Thameside tugs. When we finally crossed the river into Kent it was like a journey into Hades itself. On that particular day the Garden of England turned out to be just as pea-soupy as Essex was – perhaps more so! We drove slowly, ever so slowly, through the grey-enveloping countryside until we eventually came to the Medway Valley just above East Farleigh. Somewhat predictably we got lost.

Slasher got out the map but not knowing exactly what road we were travelling on at the time found it less than helpful. Obscured by the clammy weight of the swirling fog something with the apparent shape of a man loomed up ahead of us. "Ask him where we are," Slasher commanded, in an authoritarian manner. "Go on Dibs, ask him." Dibs unwound the window. "Could you tell us where we are," he ventured, timidly. And silence was the sole reply. "Ask him again," suggested Slasher, "go on!" Dibs asked the vague, misted, apparition time and time again, but still to no avail. All was fog and exceptionally eerie silence. "Get out of the car," I proposed, somewhat hopefully, "go over and talk to him face to face." "Frigg off!" was the less than reasonable response, " if you think I'm going out there then you've got another think coming; it may be the reincarnation of Jack the bloody Ripper for all I know." And he didn't know much poor Dibs – not very much at all! "All right, I'll go," I said, exhibiting the sort of foolhardy bravery I was less than famous for, "I'll go!" I snuck up to the diminished and dissolving doppelganger in the mist and whispered my request through quivering lips. Nothing – not even "piss off you irritating little oik!" I crept closer and peered into the obfuscating results of November's shivering dew-point. The apparition was blue from head to foot. Seized by uncontrollable terror I was petrified – rooted to the spot! A fitful breeze stirred the dank, grey, enveloping miasma and slowly all was revealed as the curtains parted. It was a police telephone box!!! A frigging police telephone box!!! A mixture of relief and utter embarrassment loosened the stone in my boots and sent me scurrying sheepishly back to the car with the unhelpful news of my one and only 'close encounter of the third kind'! Eventually, more by luck than judgement I should add – we found our way to the river. East Farleigh in the autumn is a roach fisher's paradise. I've fished Teston, Wateringberry and Barming, but East Farleigh was definitely my favourite stretch of the Medway. It had everything: weirs, locks, slow water, fast water, deep bends, deep holes and shallow glides. Sometimes we fished above the lock in the stillest water. That was Chucky's favourite spot and one where a good mixed bag of fish could be had. I preferred to walk eastwards along the river, under the trees and out into an open meadow, where the river was faster and shallower and perfect for autumn roach and chub. Elderberry Lane I used to call it – Elderberry Lane! On that particular November day I was in for a session to end all sessions! The fog cleared to a calm, blue, humdinger of an autumn day. Up until about three-o-clock in the afternoon I had very little in the way of fish to show for my efforts: a few small roach and dace, but nothing else of consequence. And then it happened – as it often does unexpectedly and unaccountably. The fish came on to feed. The river was only partially coloured and I could see the roach and chub turning with a flash of their silvery flanks to take my loose feed on the edge of a gravel bar. It was magic!!! I couldn't fail. Prime and perfected roach and chub of a pound or more in weight came to my waiting net at increasingly regular intervals. Believe it or not, in what time there was left to me before it got dark, I emptied and refilled my keepnet three times! Admittedly keepnets were much smaller in those days, but even so it was one of the best sessions I'd ever had – before or since. It was fantastic. On another occasion when we were fishing in the swirling waters below the weir with small perch floats, larger hooks, and lob worms for bait, Pancho caught a wild brown trout of about three pounds – and what a fight that beast gave him! You may not believe it but in those turbulent waters, even when cloudy after rain, I've caught some wonderful roach on what would otherwise seem very unsuitable tackle. Needless to say when we fished in that racing torrent it was perch that we were really after. If you let the float race through and then settle in the slacker water at the tail of the weir where the food congregated – small fish, worms, hook baits or whatever – you would invariably get a take. And good wholesome perch they were too: half a pound, a pound, a pound and a half; fantastic hard fighting fish.

The Medway wasn't the only river we fished in Kent. The Kentish Stour was another favourite location. We particularly liked Grove Ferry and Plucks Gutter. Being as they were much further to the east – near Canterbury – we usually made it a full weekend session and camped overnight next to the river. Grove Ferry was our most often chosen destination – mainly because of the proximity to the pub! Many a boozy night was spent in that particular hostelry regaling each other with tales of the monsters that got away, and as the night progressed even the fish that we'd caught increased in size at an alarming rate! In proportion to the proliferation of pints – no doubt! The river there was tidal and had a selection of small promontories sticking out into the water. This was where the 'juniors' fished. The best, deep swims, between two overhanging willows were reserved - if that's the right term – for Slasher and Denny. I couldn't wait to grow up in those days; I was convinced that increasing age and the size of fish were inextricably linked! The river at Grove Ferry wasn't exceptionally wide and you could easily float fish the middle track – despite the strength of the tide – if you used fairly heavy tackle and a float buoyant enough to be held back against the flow. Sometimes if I felt in a lazy mood I ledgered – which itself could produce excellent results – but usually I and everyone else stuck with their float gear. On one occasion - when peering mindlessly into Slasher and Denny's swims – I saw a fish with all the bulk and length of a large log torpedoing its way upstream. What it was I couldn't tell you for sure. I assumed that it was a giant sea trout – but whether or not sea trout come into the particular river is something probably only the locals could tell you. Whatever, it gave my watery appetite the boost it need and I found myself hungrier that ever where big fish were concerned. Alas it was not to be! As usual Slasher and Denny caught the biggest fish. Surely this proves my age and fish size theory? What they caught were bream. Great hulking, bronze slabs, the size of those proverbial dustbin-lids. You might think that envy is not a part of my piscatorial repertoire – but you'd be wrong; very wrong!!! I was as green-eyed as all the grass in the Land of Blarney. I could have killed for fish like that – and still would if it wasn't for the yellow streak running right up the middle of my back! The bream they caught – and there were many of them

– were all around six or seven pounds in weight; and back then such fish were considered to be specimens indeed. All I caught on that particular day – apart from a few roach that seemed more like roach/bleak hybrids that anything else – was a cold! Remember the promontories sticking out into the tidal river? Well, the one I was fishing from decided to become an island as the tide began to rise – a floating island at that! My 'comrades in rods' – insensitive brutes that they were – thought it extremely funny to see me and all my tackle drifting out from the bank and into the panic-inducing danger zone – cretins!!! The one thing I've learnt about floating islands, is that they don't stay floating for long. The inevitable happened and I sank with all hands, feet, rods, bait, hooks and sandwiches. Begrudgingly, the guffawing multitudes threw me a line and saved me from the clutches of dear old Davy Jones! Probably the only reason I got any assistance at all from my worm-dangling associates is because the thought of all the fishing time wasted in having to attend an inquest was too painful to contemplate!!! I managed - with the aid of an improvised grapple to retrieve most of my tackle – and then stripped off and stood naked and shivering on the bank while the 'kindhearted' Slasher went to get a flea-bitten, foul-smelling, dog-haired, car blanket to hide my embarrassment and goose pimples the size of ostrich eggs. Such are the joys of angling my friends – such are the joys!

The only other freshwater havens of note we fished in Kent were the Royal Military Canal and the River

Rother – both excellent venues I have to say. The marshland in Kent and the marshland in Essex have much in common: sheep, wind, wide cloud-swept skies, and a sparkling, reticulate web of inviting waters. The Military Canal was renowned for its tench but needless to say – my 'incompleteness' as an angler being the watchword – I personally never caught any. Gibbo the Tench did of course – sickeningly often in fact. I did catch roach. I'm beginning to think that I must have been a roach in a former existence! But they were lovely, carefree days, with many a mixed bag of scaly, river smelling, sinewy delights to show for them. The Rother was a different proposition altogether. Often clear in the summer it was best fished after rain when it was just beginning to fine down. When the conditions were right if you trotted your swim correctly you could expect a very good weight of small roach, dace and chub indeed – with a fair number of better fish mixed in amongst them. Roach – how many times have I mentioned those delightful, pink-bellied, aromatic, very personifications of angling itself? Nowadays carp and barbel seem to be all the rage, but then, well, a two pound roach was the *raison d'etre* of every angler's existence. We dreamt of roach in those days: not sixty pound carp, twenty pound barbel, ten pound chub or twenty pound bream. No, a two pound roach would have authenticated the existence of any fisherman worth his salt – size isn't everything; as the duchess didn't say to the bishop! BIG, BIG, and even BIGGER; that's all you hear nowadays. Not me. I like to hook into a double figure carp the same as the next man – but there are limits surely? Fishing for me is about the total experience and as far as I'm concerned roach, dace, chub, perch, tench, bream and crucians, are as welcome in the landing net – or to hand if they're small enough – as any amount of named carp and well known, oft caught, river rounded barbel. I mean no offence to the specimen men amongst you but we seem to be obsessed with weight. For me it's not just the weight of the fish – although that's important. In fact it's not even solely about fish at all! It's the experience of going fishing: the environment, the tactics, the sunsets and sun rises, the camaraderie or the isolation, the weather, the wildlife, the watercraft and all the bonhomie and blarney about the days catch in the pub afterwards. As I said, for me it's a total experience, it's both primitive and sophisticated, subjective and objective, relaxing and energizing. But most of all it's fun!!! Or it should be. The antis would have the rest of the world believe that we're just atavisms; throw backs to a more primal, cruel and carnivorous age. Nonsense!!! We've already seen much of the countryside turned into one vast, green factory; and now those who enjoy nothing more than looking down the end of a long, wagging finger at the rest of us 'lesser beings' would like to see the rest of it turned into a natural history museum! Well, not for me, I'm a participator, not an observer. I have canines and incisors and I'm quite happy to use them when I feel the need. But when vegetarians and vegans accuse me of cruelty - especially where freshwater fishing is concerned – then I can be just as self righteous in my own intransigent way. Where conservation and fish welfare are concerned the average club angler – and many who fish the commercials – know more about and have more care for fish and the environment than all the town and city orientated, moralizing, do-gooders put together. I rest my case! It's now time to leave Kent, my hysterical ravings, and the joys of freshwater angling – for the time being at least. Sea angling and coarse fishing were two sides of the same watery coin as far as me and my friends were concerned. We invariably alternated between the two and enjoyed both equally. The next chapter will concentrate on the seawater environment of South Essex: the creeks, the estuaries, the deeps, the piers, jetties and beaches. Break out the boat rods and the beachcasters, sharpen your hooks, put heavier line on the spool and dig yourself some lugworm. The cod are biting my friends; cast up-tide, get the landing net ready, pump like you've never pumped before!!!

CHAPTER FIVE

SEAWEED – SAND - AND SALTWATER

Living in Pitsea meant that we were only ten steam-haunted, iron-railed miles, from Southend-on-Mud – as it was so affectionately known. Being – as we were – at the bottom of the pecking order, mine and Pancho's piscatorial responsibilities lay in the direction of bait digging. If we were all going to fish Southend Pier on Sunday, then Saturday would see us equipped with two forks, a bait-box, and the return rail fare to the seaside. I didn't mind bait digging, though not being quite as big and strong as Pancho I tended to be more of a procrastinator than a practitioner where the mud-squelching, fork-bending arts were concerned! This didn't go un-noticed and I was invariably admonished for my indolence! "Isn't it about time you dug some bloody worms?" said the boy with a JCB as an ancestor, "you lazy, useless, bastard!" "I'm applying fieldcraft," I replied, somewhat inappropriately considering the tidal terrain! "Brains are always better than brawn in a situation such as this." Why didn't I ever learn to keep my mouth shut? "I'll give you brains," he thundered, lunging towards me with four sharp prongs and a look unwholesome enough to shrivel the largest of adolescent testes! Before you could say Jack Hargreaves I was nose down, arse up, and doing my bit for the Angler's Benevolent Society! Discretion, as they say!!! Lugworm were relatively easy to come by in those days, just look for the worm casts and get stuck in, but ragworm were a different proposition altogether. Usually there were two small holes in the mud, a foot or two apart, and their tunnel was a deep U shaped bend connecting the two apertures. You dug slightly away from the holes so as not to cut the ragworm in half. When you eventually located your quarry – in the face, so to speak – there was another little problem to overcome. They had pincers like frigging can-openers!!! "You pick it up Pancho," I'd say, hopefully. "Piss off," would come the uninhibited reply, "you do it!" And do it I invariably did; always with a certain amount of fear and trembling on my part, I have to admit – shamefacedly. Crabs had their own metal-rending appendages but for some reason they didn't seem to frighten me as much as ragworm. Perhaps it was because they were easier to handle; a finger and thumb either side of the carapace just above the protruding eye balls, and you were safe – hopefully! It wasn't the normal rock-hard, green shore crabs that we were after. We wanted them when they were either about to shed their shell – peelers – or after they'd already shed it – softies. We'd usually find them in the bladderwrack next to the wooden groins and by the concrete walls of the saltwater swimming pools. You could also get them straight from the ooze if you were observant enough. Look carefully and you'd just see their eyes peering above the mud and a vague outline of their shell. The one you picked up was invariably an ordinary hard backed shore crab, but often, nestling underneath you would find a softie. Even crabs it seems have protective feelings towards their kith and kin. Not that it did them much good – sadly. At least, not where we were concerned! Something that your average land-lubber wouldn't understand is the speed at which the incoming tide travels across the mudflats. I've known it to move at almost walking pace and it doesn't always go in the direction you expect it to! There are many gullies and depressions in the ooze off of the Southend and Westcliff shoreline. Many's the time I've looked up from digging bait only to see a vast expanse of shivering water between me and landfall. It was all part of the experience. Wading waist deep in the briny with a fork and bait box lifted above one's head all added to the adventure – if not to the circulation! Having – as I still have – a somewhat vivid imagination, I used to think of myself as a native porter wading across the upper reaches of the Zambezi – trying all the time not to think about crocodiles! Happy days! In the summer it was mostly black headed gulls screeching in the salt laden wind or little terns diving for fish in the sun-shot waters of the Ray, but in autumn and winter it was a veritable menagerie of waders, passerines, and wildfowl. Passerines were made up mostly of starlings and crows with the occasional rock pipit. Starlings, which roosted in the trees along the cliffs, would forage along with the crows over the mudflats. What they were feeding on I couldn't tell you exactly, but both being very much opportunists, I'm sure they ended up crop-full and very contented. The rock pipits bobbed and flirted their tails beside the groins and concrete walls and were probably feeding on sea lice, sea skaters, and other delightful water borne delicacies! The dark-bellied Brent geese started to arrive at the end of September: great long, loose, unwritten lines of language, telling of frost and snow and razor sharp easterlies all the way from far

Siberia. Their black, cacophonous, aerial journeyings, sounded like all the hounds of hell following the Devil as he hunted with the Four Horse Riders of the Apocalypse! Curlew carved the cooling air with their calls and the end of the world seemed eminently possible. In February at dusk – and on into the night – the widgeon whistled their eerie nocturne, and swans would descend from their seventh heaven in the dark, like annunciating angels; but enough of all these avian delights – as pure and pleasurable as they are – and back to the fishing.

Southend Pier was – before the deprivations of the trawling industry – a wonderful place to fish. Along the stem to landward you would catch flounders, eels and plaice mostly. Towards the station at the seaward end there was an area specially noted for garfish and mackerel. On the eastern side of the station you were always in with a chance of catching a decent bass up to five pounds or more and plaice of enormous proportions were known to find their way into the waiting drop-nets! Softies and peelers accounted for most of the best fish – though ragworm had its days! Close to the end of the pier you could go down onto one of the lower decks – away from the day-trippers – and fish between the piles for shad, horse mackerel, and grey mullet. At the very end of the pier itself – where the pleasure boats, such as the Medway Queen and the Royal Daffodil landed – you could catch – depending of the season – pouting, whiting, channel whiting, codling, cod and various other oddities such as the large headed, monstrous apparition, known as the angler fish. Eels at the right time of year could be caught almost anywhere and jellied or stewed straight from the salt seasoned sea were of course – delicious. The only species that caused any real problem were the great and lesser weever fish! These had venomous dorsal spines and could cause a very painful wound if not handled carefully. In those days the 'urban myth' was as prevalent as it is now, and stories of dying in excruciating agony only minutes after being stung by one of those vicious little brutes – abounded! Needless to say – being the pusillanimous wimp that I was, and still am, incidentally – I was often known to cut my line rather that to come into personal contact with those offending little creatures from the deep! Our favourite spot on the pier was definitely East Point. There the main quarry was dabs. Wonderful sweet tasting flatfish that make up for in flavour what they lose in size. In those days you could catch them by the sack-load! I'm not joking – honestly! The water was alive with seals diving to partake of Neptune's seemingly eternal feast. Porpoises leapt from the sea in black and silvery shoals and the sunlight turned the murky waters of the estuary into a blue and golden tropical paradise. We usually fished with fairly stout pier rods – being as we needed to cast a considerable distance – and used five pound hook lengths on a paternoster connected to ten pound main line. In neap tides or at slack water you could get away with a very light lead, but in springs or when the rip was gathering at a pace you needed at least four ounces. Mind you, boat fishing out in the Middle Grounds, I've been known to use more than half a pound of lead!!! Let's get back to East Point. No sooner had you cast in than you had your first knock. We soon learned to leave things as they were and wait for another two bites. More often than not you'd bring three fish up at a time! They were lovely little dabs ranging from about eight ounces to a pound in weight. Very tasty!!! On one particular day me and Slasher, Dibs, Chucky and Pancho, caught so many in just a couple of hours that we decided to pack up early for fear that we would not be able to carry them all back to the pier train! What did I say about trawlers decimating fish stocks? It might well be a case of the P calling the K, B – don't you think? Anyway, that was Southend Pier in those days and although it's nowhere near as prolific nowadays I'm reliably informed that there are still some good fish to be had – ALLELUIA!!!

Apart from Southend Pier we often fished the creeks around Hole Haven – to the west of Canvey Island – for eels and flounders. Slasher was a building maintenance foreman for the Mobil Oil Company. They had their own fishing club and much to our delight a boat moored from a work's jetty near the Fobbing Horse, that Slasher – and more importantly – WE, were allowed to use. It was a beautiful boat, probably 30 foot long with a beam of about 8 foot or more. Built of marine ply, it had a wheel house, a cabin, and a large inboard diesel engine. It was named the Pegasus. This I put down to synchronicity – a meaningful coincidence. Pegasus in Greek mythology was the horse that kicked a hole in Mount Helicon with its hooves, from whence issued the spring known as the Hypocrene. This particular spring was supposed to be the wellspring and inspiration of all poetry. Having since had four collections of poetry published myself I now see this early manifestation of the mythical horse as very portentous indeed! I bet you love a smart arse – don't you? Enough you cry! ENOUGH!!! And you're probably right. Flounders and eels – the creeks were knee deep in them – you just couldn't go wrong. We often used to fish all night off the mooring – seeing no need to venture out any further. What an eerie world it was. What with the lights of Canvey on one side across the wide and desolate marshes and the lights from the refinery and the flares – stacks for burning off excess gases – reflecting in the moon splintered water, it had all the props required for a vampire-ridden Hammer Horror Movie! We caught lots of eels and flounders in those waters – mostly on light tackle; freshwater spinning rods, or even float fishing for the flounders with a match rod – and some of the flatfish and the spirits of the Sargasso, weighed more than 2lbs! We even caught a number of school bass just about large enough for the pot. But it has to be said, sadly, that most of the fish we caught there were virtually inedible. There was so much oil spillage in the area that fish – especially bottom dwellers, like eels and flounders – were infused with the noxious fluid. Still, they didn't seem to be keeling over from the experience, and because of their 'crude-induced' tastelessness we put most of them back to live another day. What gentlemen we were! About 500 yards from the jetty to the south there was a warm water outfall. On warm summer days Pancho and I would sometimes walk along the seawall with our tackle and see what we could hook. Fish there were in plenty taking advantage of the warm water. At times you felt as though you could have walked across the backs of all the assembled bass and mullet. Big fish too – monsters, nay, leviathans!!! We tried floats, spinners, spoons, and freelining, but those fish were wary and elusive – and that's for sure. Over a period of time we caught a number of the smaller bass and mullet – and great fun it was too – but never managed to hook into any of the lumps! Others did, but only by the dubious method of fishing with a weight and a line full of trebles – not my idea of sport; not then, or now for that matter. We did occasionally take the boat out – not very far admittedly – but far enough for our piscatorial purposes. The first time we took it out we anchored off in the mouth of Hole Haven Creek a few hundred yards to landward of a deep water buoy marking one of the navigable channels in the Thames. To the east was Canvey Island and a pub known as The Lobster Smack – mind you, I've never seen a lobster caught in Hole Haven Creek; but that's another kettle of conundrums – is it not? Incidentally, the pub has an ancient lineage; it was once mentioned in Charles Dickens' Great Expectations as the site of some bare-knuckle fighting. Far too macho for me I'm afraid!!! Having anchored off and started to fish we were suddenly surprised by some hollow knocking sounds from down below the decks. Was it mermaids bumping their breasts against the barnacles - Neptune knocking his tripod against the hull to stop us from falling asleep in the warm summer sunshine? No, it was neither! The tide was going out and we were running aground! There was nothing that we could do about it – it was too late. Before we knew it we were high and dry on a sandbank with the two prongs of Hole Haven Creek sticking out into the River Thames on either side of us – how embarrassing! The summer holidaymakers lined up along the seawall with pints in their day-tripping mitts thought the spectacle of a boat-load of red-faced anglers wandering about on the sandbank with their hands in their pockets and their shoulders shrugged, to be very amusing indeed. HEARTLESS MORONS!!! "Hoist the main brace! Weigh anchor! Hard a port!" and other less than welcome nautical remarks drifted on the salt-laden winds in our general direction. Being something of a fan of Robert Newton and Treasure Island I responded with such sea-salted expressions as: "Belay thy tongue! Stow e gab! And shut the fuck up!" - Being, as I undoubtedly was - out of bare-knuckle range. Eventually – as is the way with all lunar events – the tide returned; albeit belatedly. We made our slow way back to the jetty in the dark, determined to invest in charts and waterproof torches!

The seawalls of Hole Haven Creek were also ideal for eel and flounder fishing. Flounders of well over two pounds were not that uncommon there and I've spent many a pleasant summer day fishing for them with freshwater gear – either float tackle or ledger. If fishing with float you didn't have to worry too much about the rise and fall of the tide because they could not only be caught off the bottom but would rise quite a few feet through the water to take the bait. Sometimes I would wander off on my own well upstream. Not only was I – and still am – a lover of solitude, but found the peace and tranquility of the marshland waterways extremely conducive to my burgeoning career as a poet! Mindlessly gazing at a float came quite naturally to one of my disposition and an inspired imagination was usually the result of such piscatorial indolence. Sadly – being an adolescent – some of the iconography of my juvenile thoughts was not always particularly holy! Naked, nubile, young girls often interfered – to use an appropriate pun – with my tackle and tactics!!! On one hot, summer's day I found my own tenuous, wriggling worm, unaccountably increasing in size. Now, in those days it was common knowledge that I was something of a wanker – along with most of my spotty, bum-fluffed associates; and truth to tell, if put to the vote I would probably still warrant the said classification to this very day! Needless to say being a healthy young buck of the wildwoods I soon found it necessary to handle the empurpled beast. I had the seawall behind me and had taken the precaution of checking the surrounding area for signs of human occupation. There was not a soul insight – perfect. I settled back to do what the Pope defines as abominable and felt both suitably guilty and strangely excited at one and the same time. When at the point of no return I had that inexplicable feeling one sometimes gets that I was being watched! On looking up I saw a courting couple walking hand in hand along the seawall towards me. What could I do? I stuck the one-eyed hairy snake back into its lair and suffered the consequences of an exceedingly messy, uncontrollable, ejaculation. The courting couple were giggling with a frequency comparable to the increased reddening of my post-pubescent Physiognomy and my fears of being prosecuted under the 'Perversion and

Exhibitionism Act of 1984' turned the pit my Orwellian stomach into a lead-lined cavern of abysmal, palpitating despair. But did that voyeuristically terminated experience of masturbation *en plein air* teach me to desist – did it hell!! The whole of my youth could be summed up as a period of incessant 'monkey spanking' in all weathers and at all points of the extracurricular compass. Bumping into walls was an occupational hazard and the only cure would have been to have tied my hands permanently behind my back and for someone to hold up a book of simultaneous equations for me to look at instead of my normal educational diet of 'Tit Bits' and 'Health and Efficiency' magazine!!! Another consequence of being caught in *flagrante delicto* in those early days was similar to the behavioral problems I had concerning crucian carp and golden pubic hair – *ipso facto,* incongruent juxtapositionings of fish and fantasy. Now I had added flounders to my list of sexual stimulants! I couldn't look at a flounder – and still can't – without my mind becoming preoccupied with thoughts of masturbation. Once again it's only my therapist and the drug companies that are reaping the rewards of my psycho-sexual machinations. I'm not a vengeful man by nature, but I sincerely hope that that insensitive, giggling courting couple either caught a dose of the galloping clap or found themselves playing mothers and fathers for real – prematurely!!! For a book purportedly concerning itself with the intricacies of rod and line fishing there's been an inordinate amount of licentiousness in the text thus far and I think it only fair – in consideration for the more sensitive and puritanical amongst you – to return to the intended subject matter – forthwith. Hence the next paragraph – boat fishing on commercial craft in general and on one privately owned vessel in particular.

We used to board commercial craft from a slipway close to the banjo end of Southend Pier. They were good sturdy, clinker built craft with inboard engines and room for about eight anglers to fish comfortably. Using the slipway meant that you could go fishing at any state of the tide, unlike the walk across the squelching and intractable mudflats to board a private vessel – unless you could afford the luxury of a dingy of course! We fished out from Southend Pier in all seasons and all weathers – except for thick fog and gale force winds. Although it has to be said that weather forecasting with seaweed and pine cones is not the most proficient of meteorological enterprises, and we often found ourselves caught out by unexpected falls in pressure and the subsequent increase in the Beaufort scale! Although I was never seasick in the estuary or even further out into the North Sea, it was often a very close call indeed. High winds and short seas I could cope with, but the long, rolling swells that set in a couple of days after a storm were nauseating – to apply the correct nomenclature! I couldn't go down into the claustrophobic, dizzying confines below deck for fear of involuntarily filling my own rubby dubby bag! All I could do was stand on deck eating and drinking as much as I could manage whilst at the same time keeping my eyes firmly fixed on the distant horizon. Eventually all feelings of seasickness would subside and I could then get on with the job in hand –

namely, catching fish! Depending on what was being caught locally we might fish anywhere from Canvey Point through to the Middle Grounds or the Shoebury Buoy and beyond to the Maplins and the wide, open, landless spaces of the North Sea. Obviously the season of the year determined what fish we caught. Flounders and eels off Canvey Point; Cod, codling, whiting, pouting, dabs, plaice and mackerel from the Middle Grounds, similar from Shoebury Buoy with eels and school bass as an added bonus, and skate, bass, dogfish, spurdog, tope, nursehound and smoothhound from the Maplin Sands. Sometimes we'd cross to the sandy side of the river towards Kent where there was always a chance of not only catching skate or bass but also the occasional conger. Sole were also abundant in the estuary but I never ever caught one. I have subsequently been told that the best time to catch them is at night using very small hooks and bait to match - I must give it a try sometime! Although I've mentioned a considerable number of different species, it has to be said that in all honesty I never caught all of the fish in question nor unfortunately the biggest of those that I did manage to hook into, but fishing – as I've repeated *ad nauseam* – is not just about catching fish! A hot, calm summer's day anchored in one of the swatchways off of the Maplin Sands is a joy in itself. The blue-be-silvered, sparkling water; a Thames Sailing Barge drifting on the tide with its sails slack and gasping for air, or a little tern hovering above the barely rippling waters waiting to dive for its prey and shatter the sea's reflective mirror to a thousand obscuring pieces, these are the things that angling's all about – the joys that make a fishless day inconsequential.

We also fished on one particular private vessel. Melondrimple, who had started work for a local trawler company, bought himself a clinker built, double-ended lifeboat of about twenty two feet in length. It was – as its original purpose demanded – a strong, sturdy and stable craft, and we always enjoyed fishing from it. Once in November the juniors amongst us decided to leave the adults at home and do a bit of night-fishing for codling and channel whiting. This was something of an adventure as none of us had been night-fishing on a boat before without interfering adults for company. At dusk we walked across the mudflats to the mooring with the sound of redshank and curlew adding their auditory wonder to the already evocative moonlit sparkle on the distant tide. We sat in the boat, tackled up and waited for the waters to rise. Although apparently clear, a fog horn began to the augment the isolate atmosphere with its mournful, repetitive tones. The Chapman Light flickered on and off as swathes of gold revolved and diminished in the cold night air. This was something special; a 'night to remember'! The boat gradually lifted, bumped bottom a few times, lifted again, and then finally was afloat. We let go of the mooring as the engine puttered into life and moved off towards the Middle Grounds and the waiting fish – hopefully! When we arrived at our destination we dropped anchor in a few fathoms of water close to the main shipping channel – and there we sat, rising and falling gently on the slight swell. The fish were very obliging on that particular night. Fishing light with running ledgers and long traces we were soon into some big channel whiting – two pounds or more a piece! Eventually the codling also turned up

– three, four and five-pounders coming over the side at a satisfying rate. And then it happened; as if out of nowhere the fog descended – the thickest, dankest, grey pea-souper that you've ever witnessed. We didn't know here we were but fortunately we were experienced enough not to panic. Having no chart or compass – not that experienced perhaps – we decided to stay put and sit it out. As I mentioned before we had dropped anchor close to the main shipping channel and before long ships of unknown tonnage started to pass us in their fog-shrouded invisible way with fog horns blaring – it was terrifying! We sat there all through that shivering night waiting to be hit amid ships and to be sunk with all hands! I've been frightened many times in my life but that was something else. On occasions we could actually see the great, looming hulls of the ships as they passed by rocking us dangerously with their wash. Eventually a breeze picked up and the fog began disperse. But as they say 'time and tide wait for no man'! Although we could now see the shore lights the tide was on the ebb and we didn't know whether or not there would be enough water for us to make it safely to the mooring. We crept gingerly landwards but before we were in sight of the mooring we started to bump bottom. There was only one thing for it – somebody had to get out and walk! You've guessed. Whimpering was to no avail, I was volunteered and that was all there was to it. Mind you, as Archimedes theory came into full play and the vessel continued to bump bottom, all the assembled crew had to disembark and join me in the icy waters of a cold and frosty late November morning. There is some justice in the world after all – praise be to God!!! You'd have thought that we would have learnt something about the arts of navigation after our experience of running aground in Hole Haven Creek – wouldn't you? Unfortunately our learning curves – and especially mine – seem to traverse further than the very ecliptic of the moon itself and we were lucky to find ourselves still alive – LUNATICS!!! Mind you, we did invest in a compass and a chart of the Thames Estuary after that decidedly unfortunate experience and never again suffered the ignominy due to those who ignore the rules of the road and the perils of the sea.

To continue our tour of the Thames estuary we'll concentrate on the beaches, bastions and jetties that gained our attention with the tales of the big fish that inhabited their tidal depths and of the leggy and bus-full loose women who promenaded along the seafront both by day and by night! You could fish anywhere along the beach from Chalkwell in the west to Shoeburyness in the east. Obviously, Being as Chalkwell was further up river than Shoebury the tidal range was considerably less. If you wanted to catch predominately flounders you went west, but if plaice were your quarry you went in the opposite direction. I find both flounders and plaice very much to my culinary liking. Some people wouldn't give a flounder to their cat as think they taste both bland and muddy, but I've found that if you take the precaution of scraping the congealed blood from their backbones – they fry up rather nicely, thank you! But even I, when push comes to shove, prefer the taste of plaice so, I invariably fished for them from the Thorpe Bay

Bastion to the east between Southend and Shoeburyness. And beautiful orange-spotted flatfish they were too. Out from the bastion there were unnumbered acres of mussel beds and the plaice seemed to like them to the exclusion of almost anywhere else at some times of the year. Whether this was for feeding or spawning or both I'm not really sure, but we certainly took our share of prime fish from those hallowed waters – and people still do I'm told! Camper Road Jetty; now there's a name that conjures up many an episode concerning my - and my friends - misspent youth. Under the pretext of fishing I would load up my 650 BSA Gold Flash combination with tackle and provisions and head off with the rest of my motorcycling friends in the direction of fun – sometimes fish – and unspeakable frolics! Camper Road Jetty had an all-night café opposite, the Castle pub on one side, and the 77 motorcycling club and general den of iniquity on the other – paradise indeed! We would chat up the ladies of the night in the café, trying to get our ends away for free, under the guise that we hadn't yet lost our cherries! It didn't work unfortunately, but it was a great crack all the same. One of our motorcycling friends and his moll were insatiable where sex was concerned – in fact I've even seen rabbits blush just at the mention of their names! There was a boardwalk by the beach and they often utilized its nether regions – excuse the terminology – for their sexual gymnastics. Through the gaps in the walkway we could see his bare backside as it thrust into her erogenous zones and pumped up her ejaculating vocal chords! "Oooh! O! Oooh! Ah! Faster! Slower! Faster! Slower! I'm coming! I'm coming! I've come! Oooooooooh!!!!!!!" Ah – Happy days! What's this all got to do with fishing I hear you say – well, you know the problems I had with crucian carp and flounders; so what do you expect – Mr. frigging Crabtree? Between the booze in the Castle, the harlots in the all-night café, and the shenanigans in the 77 club, we did occasional dangle a line or two. Camper Road Jetty was a great place to fish. Plaice and flounders were plentiful, eels and school bass were abundant in their season, and there was always the chance of something larger taking your hook bait unawares. One calm, moonlit night – or more correctly the early hours of the morning – Pancho hooked into something massive. He fought and pumped the beast for a good twenty minutes before we even got a glimpse of it, and even then it wasn't much of a sighting. All we saw in the dark, moon-silvered glow was an enormous expanse of whiteness. It could have been the undersides of a skate or even a giant plaice, but supposition was all we were left with as the monster turned, flipped its tail and dislodged the hook! Such is life – such is fishing, but there are always more fish in the sea so they say; always more fish in the sea!!! On another occasion we experienced more of 'the things that go bump in the night' variety. It was dark, pitch dark and moonless. I was sitting with my legs dangling over the side of the jetty, thinking of nothing in particular – excepting perhaps where the next fish was coming from – when something grabbed my leg! I couldn't swear to it but it felt like teeth to me! I looked down into the water – nothing. I looked behind me to see if my friends were playing a practical joke on me – it seemed not. In the split second it took to carry out both of the aforementioned procedures I was simultaneously emitting a blood curdling scream. "What the fuck!" cried the assembled piscators in unison as they headed – with as much traction as they could muster, I might add - for dry land. I was still rooted to the spot, expecting to be dragged down and abducted any second by some grotesque, scaled and slimy alien from the eternal deeps of my especially vivid imagination. What it was I'll probably never know: a seal perhaps - a toothy, sex-starved mermaid with a penchant for skinny, hairless, post-pubescent legs – a gay Neptune coming out of his watery closet at last? Who knows – I certainly don't! The time has come – as the walrus so mellifluously said – to think of other things; or more correctly, other places. The Thames estuary and its environs were – and still are – magical areas for the sea-haunted amongst us; but as with my early freshwater river fishing it was time to go further afield. By this time I and my compatriots were all fully fledged teddy boys with enough money for boat fishing, pier and beachcasting, and camping holidays on the Downs between Dover and Deal. So break out the tent pegs and the wooden mallet and get ready for some booze, bass and interminable blarney!

INTERLUDE

FISH POEMS

CARP

Shadow of the far monastic –
Stirring the fathoms of our contemplation.

Father of fishes in the thoughts of men –
Deep to the drama of our intuitions.

Spirit of lost spells –
Charmer of children in a well of wishes.

Abbot in armour at the Dissolution –
Guarding the secrets of a past conviction.

Notion of darkness – basker on the breath of night:
Totem of answers to the Holy Word –
Celled in the silence of the soul's inception.

PIKE

Sleight of the river's hand –
Hidden from yellow by the trick of green.

Long as the legend of its own illusion –
Streaming the shadows of a grown suspense.

Master in the art of bluff – raiser of unequal limits –
Fixer of fortunes through an eye of shuffles.

Riddle and answer to the weighted coin –
Tailing the caller with a head of teeth.

Prial of quick fins –
Trigger of chances in the stack of odds:

Knave in the knowledge of the winner's pack –
Dealing disaster from a sleeve of aces.

TENCH

Doctor of the dawn eye –
Tempting the sleeper into bats and birdsong.

Twitcher of tall reeds –
Telling its story with a line of bubbles.

Lover of bran and dried blood:
Mixed to the wriggle of dissected worms –
Moulded by handfuls into bombs that splatter.

Mud-puncher – sludge-shifter:
Freer of black leaves –
Lifting in layers to a seething surface.

Nerve-nudger – tester of slow curves –
Taut with the tension of unearthly power.

Bringer of portents from the louring light –
Mucus and olive in a thrash of crystal.

CHUB

Denizen of deep pools –
Rooted to hollows and the leaves of alder.

Swallower of small voles – frog slurper:
Knower of cheese in slow chunks –
Easing its yellows through a gash of sunlight.

Raiser of rashes in a claw of nettles –
Drawing the fisher to a web of tangles.

Receptor of the sudden shadow –
Cast at an angle to the edge of wild.

Spate-sucker – mud-blower:
Gawker of enormous gape –
Rounding its rubber to the nub of glutton.

Hook to the holder of the sifted pan –
Bending the barbless to a rush of fevers.

Tainter and tarnish on the name of gold –
Pumping in plunges to abysmal caverns.

ROACH

Incher of thin floats –
Testing the tenor of enormous patience.

Grazer in a green world –
Hung to the waver of a green suspension.

Bellied in age to a pink-white plumpness –
Smelling on fingers like the crux of river.

Hemp-eater – wheat-sucker:
Quern to the staple in a husk of shells.

Gulper of berries under lush Septembers –
Swimmer in autumn to a roof of leaves.

CHAPTER SIX

DOVER AND DEAL

As we got older we frequently fished further afield. The words Kent and angling are almost synonymous to me and Dover and Deal were two of our favourite destinations. When I was about eighteen years old, Slasher, Pancho, Dibs, Gibbo and me pitched camp for a week at a place called Martin Mill, up on the Downs – if that isn't a contradiction in terms – between the two aforementioned towns. Close to the camp site there was an old country pub and like the elephant on its logo the hop-scented name of Fremlins was never to be forgotten. Many of the best fishing stories are 'spun' over a pint or two of best bitter and for us on that week to end all weeks we were determined not to be the exception to the rule! Dizziness and angling have always been my constant companions. If it was not to do with the vicissitudes of the wind and tide when boat fishing, then rest assured, alcohol was bound to have the same effect! But before we savour the delights of best bitter and tall tales we'd best go and catch some fish. Dover Harbour is as good a place to start as any. You could fish from the harbour arms, the pier inside the harbour, or more adventurously, take a boat out to the dividing breakwater, well away from everyone except other anglers. This we did on many occasions and caught plenty of fish to compensate for the extra costs incurred through paying for a boat trip. As is the way with most breakwaters there were two sides to fish from! Into the harbour itself; which was invariably calm and easy to fish or out into the English Channel where on occasions the swell was so great that the sea dropped thirty feet down the breakwater wall only to rise up again and flood across the top in a swirling white wash – very dangerous indeed! My preference was to fish into the calmer water for flatfish. Plaice were fairly plentiful and I even caught a turbot once – but more of that later! The strange thing about Dover is that you rarely – if ever – catch Dover sole. Lemon sole, yes, but not Dover sole! I was reliably informed that this was the case by many of the locals who regularly fished the breakwater. If anybody knows otherwise and thinks that I'm just spinning another fish orientated yarn, then I apologize – but honestly, that's what I was told. We always used to get our bait and tackle from Deal at a shop known as Dunky Finns. Now Dunky was a sea angler par excellence. He once came third in the All-England Beachcasting Championships and even designed his own rods which were sold nationwide. Usually we'd phone up for bait a couple of days beforehand and collect it on the way to wherever we were going to fish. On this particular day we'd been into Dunky's early in the morning - and as is invariably the case with anglers and tackle dealers – had the crack about where to fish and what were the best methods to employ. Dunky said that the breakwater was fishing well for Pollack and that the best way to catch them was to attach a cork to your line and just let it knock against the seawall with the action of the swell and the tide. This I did, and much to the delight and wonder of the most 'incomplete' of anglers, caught a number of good fish ranging between about three and five pounds in weight. Unfortunately no-one had told me that they needed to be gutted straight away and by the end of the day they stunk like some antediluvian drainage duct and were fit for neither man nor beast – what a waste of good, wholesome fish! Gibbo the Tench – as is the way with all lucky bastards – caught a frigging lobster!!! I'd always assumed that lobsters were red – how wrong can one be? It was grey and yellow and blue, with many another shade that I cannot now remember. Mind you, when it hit the boiling water later that night it soon took on the hue that I'd associated it with, as the embarrassment of instant death reddened its rock hard equivalent of cheeks! On the seaward side of the breakwater you could catch most of the common species of British sea fish, but it did have one particular speciality – bullhuss: another member of the cartilaginous family of fish – including sharks and rays. Most of these fish whose skeleton is made up of cartilage instead of bone: dogfish, tope, smoothhound, spurdog, nursehound, etc. are lumped together by the fishmonger's trade and called either rock eel or rock salmon. You'd think that such beautiful fish as these would at least be accorded the dignity - especially in death - of being referred to by their proper name - you would think!!! On that particular summer's day it was hot, dead calm, with just the slightest hint of an easterly breeze. As the afternoon moved on the August haze thickened into a sea fog. It was glorious. The castle on the cliff top rose out of the sun-shot, silvery fog, like a dream of Atlantis. Sirens and fog horns sounded with all the sonorous, mournfulness of lost primeval sea monsters, herring gulls trumpeted, black-backs barked, and the golden shafted miasma carried the creative mind in and out of its misted, magical, focus. Days such as these are precious indeed. It's as if they've always been and always will be. As if the past, present and future have coalesced and everything's happening simultaneously. Magical indeed – mysterious – marvellous! That evening – back at camp – we put all our fish in a plastic bowl outside the tent. The three pound turbot I'd caught meant so much to me that I lifted up all the other fish and laid it –very carefully, I might add – right at the bottom of the heap. It was covered up – nothing could happen to it; surely! We washed, shaved, made a brew and knocked up some corned beef hash. Food fit for a king after a days fishing – and that's for sure. It was then time for a visit to the local hostelry to taste a quart or two of Fremlin's special beverage. Tall tales were told and short drinks were added to the repertoire. Sea legs began to buckle and lightheadedness and levity permeated the smoke-filled atmosphere. I suddenly found myself the very personification of Captain Ahab and my three pound turbot had mysteriously taken on the proportions of Moby bloody Dick!!! As I staggered around - spouting more blarney and bravado than a coach load of drunken Irishmen – my equally inebriated associates started to barrack me something wickedly. "It was a frigging minnow," ribbed Pancho, looking more like a transvestite every minute with his long hair and his rum and black stained voluptuous lips, "a frigging minnow!" "More like a postage stamp than a fish," countered Gibbo, as he lurched perilously close the edge of alcoholic oblivion, "I've seen bigger fleas." I wasn't having any of it, and with all the Dutch courage that alcohol invests one with, I threatened to punch his lights out! A big mistake on my part and that's a fact. Gibbo was bigger than me, had a greater reach, and a penchant for marmalizing people! Slasher had already had enough of our drunken, juvenile antics, and had repaired to the sanctuary of his camp-bed. So there we were, me and Gibbo giving each other the evil eye, and squaring up for the kill. Fortunately, alcohol and coordination have something of an antithetical relationship. Both of us took a swing and both of us spun off in opposite and ever decreasing circles until the ground and ourselves made contact – somewhat predictably, I might say! Pancho and Dibs suggested with a slur that we stopped pratting about and went back to the tent to sleep it off. That sounded good enough to me, even when drunk the thought of black eyes and bruised ribs is enough to sober me up sufficiently to see the futility of violence – especially with Gibbo the Tench! We got outside and the fresh air immediately struck me with the force of a knockout punch. I was out for the count. Gibbo – never one to hold a grudge – picked me up like a sack of spuds and carried me all the vomit-strewn way back to Martin Mill and the angler's canvas retreat. I slept the sleep of the dead that night and when I awoke in the morning with a mouth like a brewer's gusset and a head like a fairground galloper, I made my precarious way outside to partake of some of God's freely given fresh sea air – and it's non-alcoholic to boot!!! After breathing like a Buddha for a minute or two I remembered my turbot and decided to check it out for its true proportions. It was gone! Completely and utterly gone! I was both desolate and devastated. "What have you bastards done with my turbot?" I screamed, as the slumbering troops levitated in their beds, "where the fuck is it?" "Piss off Bagwash!" came the - for once - unified response, "piss off and let us get some shut-eye!" I wouldn't give in; I was mortified at my loss. Slasher asked them – scout's honour and all that crap – if anyone had half inched my turbot; and no came the negative reply. There wasn't much I could do about it – other than cry and stamp up and down on the spot! Tantrums being one of my specialities! It was probably foxes I was informed by my smirking piscatorial associates. Foxes my arse – I thought! Gibbo the Tench looked more sheepish than is appropriate to your average wolf and my suspicions were raised – and still are – to the utmost degree. He always had ways of getting his own back – the cunning bastard!!! Farewell my one and only turbot – FAREWELL!

In those days we fished Deal Pier a lot; in fact it was one of our most regular venues. At the pier head, apart from the ever-present slot machines and candy floss, the local anglers had there own club headquarters, and more importantly there was a bar! Fishing and fermented barley – what more could a man want? Those who could fish proficiently with a multiplier – and that left me out, unless you counted an endless succession of bird's nests an indication of angling prowess - could cast out far enough to get into the dogfish and conger eels. For me and my rusty, clanking, old fixed spool it was more a case of chuck it and chance it!!! Slasher loved whelks and always brought a large, flat net, to bait with herring pieces and lower down into the water between one of the well holes situated between the structural components of the pier. And whelks he caught, bucket loads of the ice cream twisted, rubbery counterparts to fishy chewing gum. I loved whelks too and would happily share in the pepper and vinegar sprinkled feast whenever the opportunity arose. The tide-rip under that pier could be phenomenal. I remember fishing one bitterly cold January night having to use a good 10oz's of lead to hold bottom. I've never caught the traditional cartoonist's boot but I have come close! On that snow-salted night my rod suddenly bent nearly double; I struck, and it was on. I fought that 'fish' against the tide for a goodly length of time and finally – after much skill – got it to the surface. And what was it – I'll tell you what it was. A sock – a great sand-full and sopping wet, frigging SOCK!!! To continue with tales of 'incompleteness', that very same night my rod bent double for a second time. This time it was definitely a fish, I could feel it fighting. This was a monster; I could feel it in my cartilaginous bones. It fought like a tiger on heat and after thirty furious minutes I got it within range of the drop-net. There was something decidedly odd about it though – instead of first seeing its head, all I saw was its tail! I'd foul hooked the bloody thing! And what was worse, the man fishing next to me, who'd had not so much as a twitch on his rod; reeled in his line until HIS rod bent double and he lifted the fish's head clear of the water. A twenty pound cod – and it was his, all his, not mine! One hook in the tail and one in the mouth; and we know whose was whose – don't we? There's a syndrome in our family known as Linford's Luck; and needless to say I was never immune from the complaint. Do you know, that ungrateful angler never even offered me the offal from the fish's head – let alone a prime fillet. Miserable git! My faith in humankind has always been prone to disillusionment, but that tight-fisted excuse for a proponent of the saltwater arts, takes the proverbial, bloody biscuit!!! We also boat fished at Deal. Once in June or July, Slasher and Pancho and I went down on our own. We hired a boat to go skate fishing and before we journeyed out to the Goodwin Sands we stopped off to do a spot of mackerel fishing for bait – and there we stayed! I've known nothing like it – before or since. We were using seven hook feathered traces. More often than not the lead never even hit the bottom. We were catching good sized mackerel – well over a pound a piece – seven at a time! If you've never experienced ten pounds of multiple mackerel fighting in all directions and thrashing on the surface like demented glass blowers, then try it for yourself – it's brilliant! We caught over five hundred mackerel on that particular occasion. Nowadays I wouldn't do it, but then we thought that the fish stocks would last forever – if we ever though at all that is – and fishless, thirty five pound a day boat trips were inconceivable. Such is the cruelty of time – and over fishing. We had our photographs taken and they graced the entrance of the pier for the rest of the summer. Fame at last I thought – fame at last; the 'incompletest' of all 'incomplete danglers' had for once excelled himself and he wasn't going to let anyone forget it – no sir, not this particular son of the sea – NO SIR!!! My first skate fishing trip out from Deal was also prone to more than its fair share of the dreaded Linford's Luck. It was a beautiful summer's day, far out of sight of land, over the oft-uncovered, golden, Goodwin Sands. I had a good, strong, solid fibreglass boat rod about seven feet long. I baited up with a fillet of mackerel and cast out a few metres from the boat. I left the anti reverse lock off of the multiplier and laid back and waited for a run. Eventually the run came. I left it for a good few seconds and then struck hard. It was on. Skate that hug the bottom are one hell of a job to shift. I pumped and I pumped and I pumped and it eventually gave way. It was about half way between where I'd cast and the boat when it surfaced. It was a beautiful thornback of about ten pounds. And then Linford's Luck took over - the screw up metal reel-seat that looked as firm as a nubile pair of breasts, suddenly gave way! The reel just spun and wobbled about uncontrollably – it was hopeless. I was reduced to wrapping my hands in cloths and pulling the line in manually. Not exactly the epitome of piscatorial elegance you might think – but what else could I do? I got the fish aboard but hand-lining a ten pound skate is not quite the same as catching it legitimately on rod and line – the sense of kudos is somewhat lacking; don't you think? Still, there you are, such is life. Mind you, it didn't taste any worse for the unconventional manner of its capture! Boat fishing from Deal was also good for plaice. Five pounders were not that uncommon and they often featured in the angling papers. One day – not far out from the pier itself – fishing with a softie on a running lead; using a Clement's Boom if I remember correctly, I had the very slightest of knocks – almost as if a crab had farted on the bait – and I struck. It was my biggest ever plaice

– and still is to this very day. It was well over three pounds and fought like a demon. A flatfish of that size is something to behold. A great orange-spotted imitation of a breakfast salver – and as white as our primal innocence underneath – phantasmagorical; magic!!! I'll finish my tale of boat fishing at Deal with a story of woe and wave engendered wonderment. Forget the lyricism – seasickness, that's what I'm talking about; nautical stomach retching! One of my favourite adults of all time – namely Denny – was a martyr to that bilious complaint. I've even seen him throw up on the beach before boarding the boat! But did that stop him going – not a bit of it. He would sit there all day as green as all the grass in County Kerry and just take it all in his stride. For me it was different. I'd never been seasick before – close, but not close enough. We boarded the boat and set out from the beach on a day as calm as the Doldrums in the fog. As time went on the Beaufort scale was gradually ascended. Moderate, fresh, strong, gale force; all this would have been more than enough to cause a certain amount of marine trepidation, but the wind got even stronger! We were all catching fish and nobody wanted to go back in. Being as it was an offshore wind the skipper was quite happy to sit it out and see how things transpired. I wasn't! Slowly but surely dizziness was turning into nausea. One minute and we were on the crest of a wave overlooking what seemed like toy boats beneath us and then we dropped like a lift without a cable into the abysmal pits of a sea-encircled hell! I started to vomit, and I couldn't stop. I near turned myself inside out on that windswept, roller coaster of a day, and just wanted to die. Did my fellow passengers have any sympathy? Did they bollocks!!! They threw a tarpaulin over me and just carried on fishing as if I didn't exist. Have you ever had your tongue and lips burnt by a surfeit of green and yellow bile? Had your throat on fire with your ring hanging on for dear life at the tail end of your epiglottis? Well, I have – and it's bloody awful! All that and a head without blood to comfort it, legs without bones, and a stomach like Vesuvius on a bad day – bloody awful!!! Eventually even the skipper started to pale and began to gibber something about Davy Jones and his ever-open locker. We went back to shore cutting the mountainous waves like a blunt and buckled knife slapping its way through an ocean of bubbling porridge. I was never so relieved in my life to reach dry land. The strange thing is that no sooner had I put my foot on the beach, than I started to feel better. I went to the newsagents, bought a bottle of lemonade, gulped as much of it down as I could in one go, and then burped the burp to end all Olympian burps! I was cured – it was as if I'd never put to sea. I've never been seasick since that blusterous and fateful day and wouldn't wish that wind-engendered trauma on anybody else. Time for some beachcasting I think – don't you?

Between Deal and Pegwell Bay was an area known as the Sandhills. To get to that particular stretch of coastline you had to cross the Royal Sandwich golf course. Incidentally Ian Flemming once lived in the area and that's where he got his inspiration for the golfing scenes in Dr No – or was it Goldfinger? Anyway, if you really want to hear some exceptionally good smart arsing; did you know that apart from writing James Bond novels, Ian Flemming also wrote Chitty Chitty Bang Bang? Strange man – don't you think!!! Enough, back to the shingle and the sussurating sea. We usually fished that beach at night as the quarry seemed to come in much closer in the dark. Although it was tidal – obviously – you could if you wished follow the sea out and fish at almost any state of the tide. We fished there through all the seasons of the year. I've been known to fall asleep on a bitterly cold, starlit, January night and wake up with my Parka covered in frost, and shivering like a jelly on a trampoline! But I loved it – really loved it! We fished – depending on the season – for codling, whiting, pouting, dogfish, conger, sole and bass, amongst others. You needed to be able to cast a 100 yards or more to get into the bigger fish. So me and my dilapidated fixed spool reel usually found ourselves well outside the frame! Never mind; the air was fresh – sometimes exceedingly so – and the exercise was good for my soul – or so I'm told! Once – in the daylight for a change – Dunky Finn came down to visit us. He had brought one of his personally designed rods with him and proceeded to give us a lesson in beachcasting. That man was a genius, an absolute genius. He didn't cast over arm like we did, but held the rod at about 45 degrees and cast sideways! The line screamed off the reel and the weight's trajectory seemed more like an orbit of the moon than anything else! The lead appeared to go on forever. I can't remember now exactly what the British record distance was, but being as Dunky had once come third in the All England Beachcasting Championships, I've no doubt that he wasn't far from equaling that achievement. Perhaps if I'd tied my rig to a floating bottle and waited for the tide to ebb I might have stood a chance – might have!!! That particular stretch of coastline was very popular with anglers. At times there were more people lined up along the beach than you'd see on the Trent in one of the Nationals! To see the masses of Tilly Lamps flickering away like a constellation of fallen stars was spectacular – not to say astronomical! On one exceptionally warm and starlit summer night Slasher, as usual, outdid all of us. He was catching sole and some of those fish would have been big enough to 'sole' the boots of any fe-fi-foing giant! It was nauseating. That man could catch fish down a drain – if he fell down the shit-house he'd come up covered in diamonds. Mind you, I was the king of the pouting, and everybody concerned dutifully revelled in that particularly unwanted accolade. It was not all warmth and whispering summer breezes by any means. I've fished full in the face of a brunt nor'easter with hard snow shot-blasting my cheeks and making my forehead ache so much that I've had to turn my back to the wind to recover my circulation and my composure. It was worth it if the cod were biting, and even if they weren't, there was a sense of experiencing the elements first hand and being closer to both nature and God than could ever be achieved wrapped up in bed and living nothing but the virtual reality of one's dreams! Once I saw a man near me jumping about and cursing in the silhouetted glow of a moonlit midnight. Bravely, for me that is, I went across to see what was wrong. His hand was covered in teeth marks and oozing a considerable amount of blood. In the dark he thought that he'd caught a dogfish, but it turned out to be a rather large conger!!! A bit too close to nature perhaps – don't you think? Sometimes the fish get their own back and I suppose it's only fair really – as long as it's not me they're targeting; that is! After the storm there is the calm. Such is the incontrovertible way of duality in this temporal realm of ours. November, and what springs to mind? Well, for me it's Thomas Hood and the eponymous and far from obscure poem he wrote on the subject of fog. One November night, too close to Halloween for comfort, and still teetering on the edge of All Souls, I had to walk back across the golf course to the camper-van to get some paraffin for the Tilly Lamps. The fog was thicker than Dibs – and that's saying something! Fear and trembling is the phrase I'm looking for I think. I was scared witless! As I walked through the swirling miasma thoughts of Jack the Ripper, Count Dracula, and other characters from Hammer's House of Horrors, flickered back and forth across my quivering neural network. Slowly, as my eyes began to adjust to the light – or should I say the lack of it – something, decidedly evil in my demented mind, started to manifest itself! I was horrified!!! I got out my torch and shone it in the direction of the evolving apparition. Who was it? Crippin, the Devil, Christopher Lee? IT looked at Me and I looked at IT, suspiciously – if you'll excuse the understatement. Then I suddenly realized what it was - a BADGER!!! By then I didn't really care what it was, I was already in need of a fresh pair of underpants and I wasn't going to hang around until I'd filled my boots as well! Old Brock seemed to be of the same opinion. Roots of stone suddenly found legs – two in my case, four in his. We both swiveled simultaneously and shot off in opposite directions towards a fog-shrouded, heart-pounding, oblivion! So much for the angler's other eye. Jack Hargreaves – what does he know? I did eventually get back to the camper-van and collect the necessary paraffin. I wasn't looking forward to wending my petrified way back across the same chilling fairways of that fog-infested golf course – but it had to be done. I started to hear some strange, rumbling, raspberry-like noises! As I got closer to the source the atmosphere was suddenly permeated by a distinct and somewhat familiar odour. Cautiously, shivering, and on the edge of apoplexy, I shone my torch in the direction of the said olfactory emanations. It was Chucky – the filthy bastard! Having been taken short he decided to go for a 'hole in one'. He'd dropped his strides above a hole on one of the greens, taken aim, and emptied his bowels directly into the diminutive aperture. Well aimed admittedly – but disgusting to the point of uncalled for malevolence. Okay, he might not have been fond of golf, but was there any need to fill that sporting receptacle with a heap of shit? Not in my book there wasn't. I don't like horse racing but I wouldn't fill Beecher's Brook with a mountain of steaming dung – would I? No, as far as I'm concerned there are limits to any form of protest; voicing one's opinions should be more than enough – surely!!! The last place I'd like us to visit in the south eastern corner of the Garden of England is St Margaret's Bay. To get there from Martin Mill you have to make the tortuous decent down - and seemingly forever down - amongst the tree-covered White Cliffs of Dover until you find yourself in a car park looking out across the English Channel, where on the clearest of days you can just about see the coast of France. There it was that we fished for bass from the beach. We would cast out beyond the third or fourth breaker, put our rods in their rests so as they were almost upright, and await the results. Crab was the favourite bait, though ragworm or strips of herring would sometimes work just as well. It was a glorious spot to fish from. Bass and summer go together, and what with the sheer, pallid cliffs behind you, the overhanging trees and vegetation, and the sometimes almost tropical blue and green of the Channel – life was definitely worth living. I'm not going to lie and say that I ever caught any monsters from that paradisal location, but I did catch school bass up to a pound or so, and occasionally something considerably larger. But as I'm so fond of saying – it didn't really matter. Just being there was enough. The sun at its blue-unbounded zenith; gulls curving and crying on the wind, coloured sails listing to the sparkling, gold-plated, leisurely horizons, and a salt-enlightened sense of infinite peace never to be found in the brick-built, concrete-girdled, precincts of twenty first century urban existence. No, if nectar's the drink of the Gods and ambrosia their food; then surely fishing must be their one and only pastime? I for one have already booked my spiritual place by the lakes, the rivers, and the sea, in the lyrical pastures of the ever-golden, ever-youthful Summerland's. Until then it's the rivers, creeks, and the tidal ways of Essex. Come with me now to some of the most sea-haunted, land-encompassed tidescapes in the whole of the British Isles. Put on your sea-boots, weigh your imaginary anchors, and get ready to set sail for bass, skate, and some of the best saltwater scenery this side of paradise!!!

CHAPTER SEVEN

PAGLESHAM PIE – BLACKWATER BASS

Creeks, tidal rivers, saltings and salt marshes are just about my favourite environment. Essex is blessed with about four hundred miles of seawall and as a consequence of this fact there is no shortage of the aforementioned habitats. The tidal River Roach – wonderful name that – connects the Thames estuary to the River Crouch. It flows between Shoeburyness and Foulness Island where it's more properly called Havengore Creek. It then passes Potton Island before joining the River Roach proper and travelling on though Paglesham until it reaches the River Crouch nearly opposite Burnham. The whole area is pretty flat and yet far from featureless. Parts of Shoeburyness are owned by the Ministry of Defense as are the whole of Foulness and Potton Islands. Sea, saltings, and extremely rich farmland are the legacy of the twice daily tides and centuries of land reclamation. Foulness once boasted two inns: The George and Dragon and The King's Head. Sadly, only The George and Dragon remains. It is a typically Essex weather-boarded building that was once the location for many illicit bare-knuckle boxing matches. The island also has a church – no longer in use unfortunately – and is famed for a makeshift road that runs next to the eastern shoreline over the tidal mudflats. This particular road is known as the Broomway and is said to be of Roman origins. It gets its name from the withies that were placed along its entire length so as it could still be negotiated even when under water! In the old days there were no roads onto the island from landward so the Broomway was very important to the island's economy – mainly in the form of sheep and cattle, arable land, and some oyster farming. It had – and still has, paradoxically, thanks to the Ministry of Defense and the subsequent restriction of access – an abundance of wildlife. As the name suggests: Foulness – i.e. Cape of Birds – is a haven for wildfowl of many different varieties: geese and ducks and waders proliferate and lately a couple of former residents have started to re-establish themselves – little egrets and avocets! It is well known for owls – especially the short eared and the barn owl. Lying on the north/south migration route it is an absolute paradise for bird-watchers – and that includes yours truly! Autumn and spring are obviously the best times to observe rarities and you never know what's going to turn up: peregrines, snow buntings, redstarts, wheatears, purple sandpipers, black terns - anything!!! Hares, rabbits, foxes, badgers, weasels, stoats, voles, shrews, rats, mice – you name it and the island supports it! Wildfowling and fishing on and around the island – where it's unrestricted of course – is as much in evidence as it has ever been. Wakering Stairs was always know for the quality of its bass fishing - and still is I'm told. But as I said earlier on in this story the mudflats can be an extremely dangerous place if you're not careful. In the 1960's three young men from Pitsea went wildfowling one cold autumnal day and while they were out hundreds – if not thousands of yards from the shore – the fog came down. Sea fogs on the low lying east coast are notoriously dense. The tide started to rise and they became disorientated. It's no use following the direction of the incoming water because there are so many currents and counter currents that it's impossible to determine exactly where the shore is in relation to the tidal flow! Sadly, the three young men drowned on that cold, clammy, autumn day, and their bodies were not all found until weeks afterwards. Where there is pleasure there is pain; where there is beauty there is ugliness. There are no answers to the tragedies this world bestows upon the unfortunate and the unwary. All we can do is be as careful as possible, pray for all departed souls, and try to transcend the darker side of this mystery we know as life! Bypassing Potton Island and its military secrets we join the River Roach proper and motor into East End, Paglesham. To the west the River Roach flows into the ancient market town of Rochford – or Roachford, perhaps – and to the north lies Burnham on Crouch. In my early days they were still farming oysters at Paglesham and you can still see the remains of the old oyster beds even now! East End hit the headlines recently. It seems that one of the old sunken hulks in a creek thereabouts is actually HMS Beagle, the very ship that Charles Darwin sailed on when he was pondering on the whys and wherefores of evolution. 'The Voyage of the Beagle' was one of the first books I ever read – closely followed by 'The Origin of the Species'. I'm still not completely convinced about 'the survival of the fittest' but one thing's for sure, the Beagle seems to have 'survived' and with a bit of luck it will be raised, restored and refitted, and hopefully become one of the Nation's treasured relics. Many years ago there were a couple of angling charter boats moored in the River Roach near Shuttlewood's Boatyard. If we wanted to fish for skate on the sandbanks off Clacton-on-Sea that was where we hired the vessel. I well remember the first time I shipped out of Paglesham. In those days there were elm trees a-plenty. Elms and the Essex marshes went together. The relatively flat landscape was counterpointed by those majestic trees. They added a rhythm to the otherwise bird-haunted silence of the diluvial hinterland. We rowed out to the boat, stowed our gear, and got ready to sail – or motor in our case! The tide was low and as we weighed anchor and started to make way all you could see on either side were the clay banks of the river towering above us. It was a strange, eerie sensation. Just the river, the wide cumulous-building Essex skies, and save for the slap of water on wood – silence! The occasional wader fluted, a shelduck laughed, but other than that – silence!! In a world where the greatest form of pollution is noise, places and moments like those are precious indeed – Silence!!! We motored out of the Roach and into the Crouch almost opposite Burnham. Burnham on Crouch is second only to Cowes when it comes to yachting. Burnham Week is famous both nationally and beyond. Yachtsmen from all points of the compass congregate on mass to sample the sailing delights of one of the best of the East Coast Rivers. The yacht clubs, the quaint, old fashioned quayside inns, the boatyards and chandlers, are all full to the gunnels with men and women of the sea, spinning their yarns and trimming their normally landlocked sails. We travelled down the Crouch – past the seals dozing on the mud banks - out of the estuary and on up through the Whitaker

Channel. It was four hours motoring from Paglesham to Clacton and I enjoyed every minute of it. Even miles out to sea the wildlife made its presence felt. Migrating birds landed on the boat for a breather. Not just birds either. Butterflies, beetles and bees, all showed up from time to time as they journeyed back and forth to the continent. Finally we reached our destination, dropped anchor, and started to fish. On that particular day the skate were more than elusive – but it didn't matter to me. I caught some nice plaice and eels and was more than satisfied. The sun was shining, the sea was blue, and the cumuli were gull-haunted and gilded by the goldsmith of the sky. What more could a man ask for? The journey back ended in the summer twilight. Flat calm - and silence – except for the flutes and whistles of the waders and the early, mournful, tu-whit, tu-wooings of the tawny owls – perfection!!! I did catch skate off of Clacton – many times in fact - nothing large admittedly, but more than sufficient for my limited needs. In the opposite direction the River Crouch wound its ever shallower way to Battlesbridge Mills. It's there that we'll stop next, have a couple of pints at the ancient Barge Inn, and talk of fishing, of times past, and times present – CHEERS!!!

Battlesbridge – contrary to its nomenclature – was not the site of a battle. It's said that the name is derived from a one time local farming family – perhaps not quite so romantic, but adequate as far as I'm concerned. When I first knew the place there were three mills, two still working and one becoming derelict. One was a steam driven mill, one an electric provender mill, and the disused one an old tidal mill. In fact, anyone with foresight could have turned Battlesbridge into the Essex equivalent of Iron Bridge in Shropshire. The complete history of tidal milling was all there in one place – what a tourist attraction it could have become! Instead, the steam mill is now an antiques centre, the provender mill has been demolished and replaced by a garden centre, and the tidal mill has been renovated – tastefully I might add – and turned into a private residence. Let's get back to the past, my past, and even earlier. When I first knew Battlesbridge the steam mill was still working and apart from coasters – whose seemingly gigantic bows towered over the road bridge – the occasional Thames Sailing Barge still worked the quay, mostly under motor power by now admittedly, but still a beautiful sight to behold. In the old days dozens of the craft would line the banks and 'mud skippers' would be employed to pole the barges the two shoal-watered, tortuous miles to Hullbridge. I read a book once about a particular spritsail barge – called 'June of Rochester'. The true story was set in the 1930's when working barges were still a common sight in the vicinity of the Thames. A couple had bought the barge and converted the hold into living accommodation. The couple worked in the city, but every weekend would pick up the barge wherever they'd moored it last and potter off around the East Coast Rivers. What a wonderful life that must have been! Salt air, the cry of gulls, listing ochre sails, and not a care in the world – wonderful! In the book there were photographs of Battlesbridge in the 30's and even earlier. The place was packed with traffic and sea going cargo. Nowadays, if you want a

Welsh Dresser or a pot plant or two, then Battlesbridge is the place for you, but if you're looking for industry and working river craft then I'm afraid you'll have to look elsewhere. Not all is lost though. The pub is still as ancient as it ever was – a little more ancient in fact – and it serves 'real ale' for the connoisseur and lager for the louts – such as my good self. On top of that people still fish the mill pool and the river itself. I dare say it's little different from my day. Eels and flounders mostly, but always the chance of a school bass or a mullet or two. It was always an interesting place to visit in winter. If you'd had a week or two of sub zero easterlies, clear skies and starlit nights, the river would invariably freeze over. I've seen plates of pure white ice a good six inches thick piled up along the seawall on many occasions. The mill pool would freeze over and if cold enough even the tidal river would be solid from bank to bank. It was a veritable Arctic scene straight out of 'Nanuk of the North'. Cold man – COLD!!! When the tide flowed in or out it would start off a debacle. The sound of ice groaning, grating, and echoing under the bridge was both eerie and exhilarating – especially at night with a full moon silvering the river and the frosted landscape. Curlew would call disconsolately and the sense of primeval isolation became almost tangible. It was as if you were back in the distant past: a hunter/gatherer, trudging wearily through the tundra in search of sustenance, scrambling over the moraine, looking and listening for wildfowl or anything else to put some strength back into your exhausted body. I digress – yet again! No, Battlesbridge was – and still is – well worth a visit. Fill a Thermos flask with soup; pack up your lightest pier tackle, and dig a few lob worms. That should do you – tight lines!

The River Blackwater and bass it seems were made for each other. Some of the biggest bass in the country have been lured in those particular salt-heavy waters and even I've had more than my fair share of their smaller cousins! When I say salt-heavy, I'm not joking or being lyrical. No, the waters around the Essex coast are some of the saltiest in the country. Evidence of this can be seen in the number of derelict salt pans there are dotted around the saltings. Aerial photographs are even more revealing! Maldon sea salt is famous world wide for its purity and flavour and is still to this day produced in bulk. Scattered around the shores of Essex are little heaps of slag-like material known as 'red hills'. These are said to be of Roman origin and are supposedly the remains of ancient salt workings. The theory is that pottery rods were made, heated by fire until red hot, and then dowsed with salt water. The water evaporated in the heat and the remaining salt clung to the pottery rods to be scraped off and utilized. That's the theory anyway! Back to the bass; we usually hired a boat from Heybridge Basin. This takes us back to an earlier chapter 'Chelmer Memories'. It's here in the Blackwater, near Collier's Reach, that the Chelmer/Blackwater Navigation and the sea make each others acquaintance. The sea lock at Heybridge Basin serves to divide the coarse fishermen form their saltwater counterparts – not that there's ever been any division in my case of course! Between Maldon and the North Sea there are three major islands: Norsey,

Osea, and Mersea. Norsey is famous for an epic Saxon battle – the Battle of Maldon. This epic event is recorded in one of the few surviving Saxon documents still in existence. A poem entitled 'Brithnoth'. Brithnoth was the ealdorman, or whatever, who stood his ground on the causeway to Norsey Island and held off the Danes – with a little help from his friends – for a considerable length of time. Although well outnumbered by the Danes, when they said that they thought it was unfair to fight on the causeway and that they would prefer to continue the conflict on open ground, Brithnoth – for reasons that are totally unintelligible to me – conceded to their request. And what was the result? Brithnoth as dead as a dumbbell, and the rest of the nation up to their necks in debt through the introduction of Dane geld! Never concede anything that's what I say – NEVER!!! Osea was, and is, something of a proper island situated as it is right in the middle of the river. It is sparsely populated, has a causeway across to Goldhanger on the north bank of the Blackwater – tide permitting – and involves itself in the local trades of farming and fishing. One of the Charrington brothers – having seen the debilitating effects of alcohol at first hand – built a house there for the rehabilitation of alcoholics – it seems that it didn't work; apparently the locals soon cottoned on to the situation and started to smuggle beer and spirits to the inmates! Capitalist exploitation I say – hoist the Red Flag; bring back the revenue men! Fish, ah yes, fish. Much as when coarse fishing, the first consideration should be the configuration of the ground beneath the water. In certain areas of the Blackwater sand and shingle bars rose up above the surrounding sea floor.

These often changed somewhat with the tides but the local skippers always knew where they were. As the tide-rip raced across these particular features the water boiled and lots of food was stirred up – and what do food and turbulent water mean? Bass – that's what they mean – BASS!!! Sometimes we'd cast straight into the turbulent water and hold bottom with heavy leads and at other times we'd use lighter weights and let the hook trundle along on and over the bars under its own momentum. Both methods caught fish – as did spinning occasionally. As I mentioned earlier, I personally didn't catch any specimens, but I've seen ten pounders hooked and boated by others and had more than enough smaller fish of my own to keep me well occupied and happy. There's nothing quite like a bass thrashing about in a shower of crystal to set the pulse racing. Beautiful, streamlined, powerful silver fish that fight like demons – determined to remain in their own watery dimension. Fantastic!!! The Blackwater was a very unpredictable river in those days. Apart from bass there were days when you could catch plenty of flatties and eels, but on other occasion it would be as dead as Dracula! I've sat there for hours without even a knock – not even a crab or a bootlace! Such is fishing. Would we enjoy it as much if we always caught a boat load of fish? I doubt it somehow. Mersea, the nearest of the three major islands in the Blackwater, to the sea, is demographically split into two halves – namely, East and West Mersea. Simple when you know how – isn't it? East Mersea is very sparsely populated and is famous for its church and its one time vicar – the reverent Sabine Baring Gould. Said vicar, not only wrote a wonderfully melodramatic novel about the area: 'Mehalah' sub titled – 'a story of the saltmarsh' – but also penned that world renowned hymn: 'Onward Christian Soldiers'. Achievement indeed – wouldn't you say? Close to the church there's an area known as Cudmore Grove. Nowadays it's a country park and I still visit the place on a regular basis. It's different to many other parts of Essex. For one thing, it's got cliffs – relatively small clay cliffs admittedly – but cliffs nevertheless! Also there is sand on the beach – another rarity where saltings predominate. For me it's always had a touch of the Treasure Islands about it. If I saw Robert Newton peg-legging his way along the foreshore with a parable on his rum-soaked shoulder – I wouldn't bat an eyelid! Robert Louis Stevenson must have visited Cudmore Grove – I'm sure of that! The way the trees grow out of the side of the cliffs and overhang the beach is so evocative of the tropics – dotted as they are with desert islands. "Shiver me timbers lad, was that a mermaid I saw frolicking in the ooze? Was that a Spanish man o war or a Thames Barge under full sail? Who knows, time and the imagination play strange tricks! To the south Mersea Island faces the River Blackwater, to the north the Pyefleet channel separates it from the mainland at high tide – apart that is from the raised roadway known as the Strood. To the east the Pyefleet Channel joins the River Colne – Colchester's salted artery – the Colne then joins the Blackwater, and the two of them eventually merge imperceptibly into the grey North Sea itself. Oysters and punt gunners seem to be West Mersea's chief claims to fame. The oyster fisheries – still thriving – are noted for their 'Colchester Natives' – delicious with paprika and a twist of lemon – Delicious!!! Every year there's an oyster festival in Colchester Town Hall – to which the rich and famous are invited, with a few free tickets left over for the proletariat to fight over! Let 'em eat cake – the oysters are ours – all ours! Strangely enough, when I was labouring for the archeologists, medieval rubbish tips were literally full to the brim with oyster shells. It appears that they were the staple diet of just about everybody – and it was the same with salmon it seems! Fashion's a funny old thing - isn't it? Gunner Musset, now there's a name to conjure with. It's a toss up as to whether he or Walter Linnet from Bradwell on the other side of the river was the best wildfowler in the area. I think I'll call it a draw before I'm crushed to death by a freefalling avalanche of Brent geese and widgeon, or torn limb from limb by rival Blackwater factions! On the other side of the river, beyond Bradwell marina, Bradwell Waterside, Peewit Island, the nuclear power station and Bradwell Village itself, there is an area known as Bradwell juxta Mare – very French, don't you think? This is one of my favourite spots on the whole of the Essex coastline. To get to the North Sea you have to park your car by a farm and walk along a track between fields of wheat, barley, or sugar beet. In spring and summer the larks lift your spirits as the lift their own cadenzas high into the lyrical, salt-elated air. They climb the rungs of Jacob's heavenly ladder until, like sun-shot angels hovering in eternity – they hang on the stasis of their own inviolable songs. At the end of the track is St Peter's Chapel. Founded by St Cedd in the 7th Century AD, it is one of the oldest ecclesiastical buildings in the country. It was built out of the remains of the Roman fort – Othona – one of the 'Forts of the Saxon Shore'. What a magical and mysterious place it is; small, barn-like – and in fact used as a barn for many years before being rededicated – and surrounded by nothing other than flat fields and water for as far as the eye can see. You could not think of another place more suited to those with the hermetic temperament: solitude, birdsong, whispering sea breezes and the sky – the wide, ever-present, wondrous Essex sky. Inside, simplicity is the order of the day: bare stone walls, dotted with the remains of Roman bricks and tiles, plain wooden benches, and a simple silver crucifix with the Christ hanging in a dignified yet painful silence. You can actually feel the spiritual presence of thirteen hundred years of Christian worship and worshippers – it's awe-inspiring, it really is! On the other side of the seawall there's an old cottage that once belonged to the aforementioned punt gunner – Walter Linnet. It and the saltings directly in front of it are now managed by The British Trust for Ornithology and I believe it's used as a bird ringing station and an observation post for passage migrants. Next to that you'll find a cockle spit facing the wide expanse of the landless northern sea. This is a favourite spot for anglers. This is beachcasting as experienced at Deal or Dungeness. Long rods, the lightest weights you can get away with, and long-distance casting are the order of the day. The relatively shallow waters still hold their fair share of fish. Most of the common species are readily caught, but the speciality from this particular beach is skate. There are not many places in the southern half of Essex where shore fishing for skate is possible, consequently the cockle spit is very popular!

I've never caught a skate from the shore myself, but then I am the self confessed 'Incomplete Dangler'. But I've seen skate caught there, and good skate at that - mostly thornback, but with the occasional common and stingray thrown in. Stingrays seem to be particularly prevalent around the Essex coast, even at times being caught well up some of the tidal rivers – especially at places like Wallasea Island on the Crouch, where large bass and mullet also like to feed along the seawall in the summer. I couldn't finish this particular chapter on the Saxon Shore without casting a line or two onto the Dengie Flats. The Dengie Flats are a few miles east of Southminster – more of which later – and are part of one of the most desolate stretches of coastline you could ever imagine. It's so shallow there, even at high water springs, that you can only fish for three or four hours – but it's worth it – it really is! Because of the tidal conditions there is a massive amount of weed growth – eel-grass, sea-grass or grasswrack – i.e. zostera marina. This in turn attracts massive amounts of fish – large bass and enormous eels mostly. To get to the flats you have to cross a pampas-like prairie of wind whispering crops and grasses. A network of dykes and sluices travel the entire length of a seemingly limitless seawall from horizon to horizon. Here and there some of the larger sluice gates have a metal gantry around them, decked out on the top with railings and timbers. These afford the solitary angler their own personal pier to fish from! One windy summer's day – even in summer a northeasterly gale can be fearsome in these parts – Pancho and I decided to go for a bit of bass fishing. We set up our beachcasting tackle on our own private pier and baited up with softies and peelers – although I'm now convinced that even hard green shore crabs would have done equally as well! Casting into a brunt nor'easter is not an easy proposition, but somehow we managed, and settled down to await results. Results were not long in coming. My rod bent down in an arc and then sprang back again. I struck and was into a good fish. It was an eel, a good two pounds in weight, and mouthwateringly handsome it was too! We continued to catch a number of eels around the same weight but felt that it wasn't going to be a day for bass. What with the wind, the lowering cloud, and the rain coming on, we decided to call it a day. I said just one more cast – and that's what we did. I as usual had nothing to show for the final cast other than limitless hope and equally limitless aspiration. But Pancho on the other hand – well! His rod was heading for Belgium when he finally caught hold of it and we knew immediately that he was into a decent bass. It fought well and by the time we saw its head shaking about in the tide we realized that such a big fish couldn't be hoisted up onto the top of the sluice. Pancho continued to play the furious fish as he carefully climbed down from the gantry to carry on the tremendous tussle right at the water's edge. The tide wasn't very deep, the fish didn't want to come in, and Pancho was in the mood for giving orders. "Take your shoes and socks off and go in after it," he commanded, authoritatively, "It's your duty as a friend and fellow angler." "You must be frigging joking!" I replied, as respectfully as possible under the circumstances, "It's as cold as the bloody Caucasus Mountains out there!" "If you think I'm joking," he retorted, still struggling with the monstrous bass, "how funny do you think it would be to have to walk all the thirty miles back to Pitsea?" Off came my shoes and socks – as well as my trousers, just to be safe! He was the driver after all! That water was cold – unbelievably cold! But the fish was tiring and I managed to grab it and drag it safely back to dry land. We never weighed it but I would estimate that it was as near to ten pounds as damn it – and what's an ounce or two amongst friends? Whatever the weight it certainly tasted exceptionally good. We had it that very night for dinner. Stuffed with butter, mushrooms, onions and tomatoes; seasoned with salt and pepper and cooked to perfection under the grill. It was delicious. Accompanied by new potatoes, fresh garden peas, white sauce and a glass of chilled white wine – delicious, absolutely delicious! So much so that I'd almost forgiven Pancho for his ultimatum concerning my good self and the extremely cold North Sea!!! Such were the days of 'Paglesham Pie' and 'Blackwater Bass'. Something happened at about that time that was to divert our attention from the local scene and to see us travelling further afield once more. Our local hostelry 'The Winged Horse' decided to get sportier and along with football, darts, and cricket formed an angling club. I for my sins – or not having the ability to say no under pressure from my peers – was elected as club secretary. The meeting is now convened – order gentlemen please – ORDER!!!

CHAPTER EIGHT

THE WINGED HORSE ANGLING CLUB

Synchronicity – now there's that strange Jungian term again. Do you remember the Mobil Oil angling boat – Peagasus? Well, here was that mythical horse again, gracing the pub sign at my local watering hole. Pegasus, who kicked a hole in Mt Helicon, thus facilitating the Hypocrene – the wellspring of all poetic inspiration! Meaningful coincidences – they abound in my life, they really do. Fate had decreed that I was to become a poet and the world in its mysterious way was forever showing me cryptic intimations of the future. I think I'll write the next chapter in rhyme – no, don't worry, I'm only joking!!! I'm not really built for committee work – never was. I'm not what you'd call a team player - more of your average self-opinionated individualist to be truthful. Why don't meetings ever seem to finish? There's always some pratt who wants to bring up some point of order – or some other banal and trivial inconsequentiality, and what's worse, they want go on for hours on the inane intricacies of the subject in question! I used to get pissed off – and still do for that matter. "With all due respect fellow member," I would propose, tactfully, "we've all got beds to go to, are you going to waffle on about nothing all bloody night?" Diplomacy was never a finer point of mine and the usual response was one of hurt pride and aggressive reaction. "Point of order, Mr.

Chairman, it's not the frigging secretary's job to close the frigging meeting!" the offended jobsworth would exclaim, whilst foaming at the lips, "he's a frigging idiot anyway!" "Rule 27," the chairman would reply, officiously, "no swearing in the club please." And so it went on meeting after meeting. Why did I allow them to pressure me into the job? I'd sooner have fished on my own in a sewage farm than fish on the Royalty with those useless cretins! But I'd made my bed, as they say, and would have to bloody well lie in the frigging thing!

The first trip I organized was a boat fishing expedition to Littlehampton. I ordered two vessels – both sixty footers – with room enough for about fifteen of us on each. We were to catch the coach at 5 am - and as was the alcoholic way with 'Mine Host' at the Winged Horse – he opened the bar well beforehand just in case anyone fancied a quick snifter! Alcohol and the ocean waves may be alright for your average old dog of the sea, but I didn't think it wise of the assembled land-lubbers to be swilling down so much grog before setting sail! Well, it was their funeral, and I was sure that Davy Jones would willingly accommodate them. We finally boarded the coach and after a seemingly interminable amount of time listening to off-key renditions of 'ten green bottles', and stopping at every bush so as the pissed-up piscators could evacuate their bladders and empty their erupting bowels, we staggered onto the waiting quayside. The wind was already fresh to strong and the scudding sou'westerly clouds and slants of intermittent rain were ominous indeed. Cloudy it was, windy it was, and wet it was certainly becoming, but it was 'summer' and the air was relatively warm, so we were tentatively optimistic. We motored out a mile or so off Beachy Head. If you think the swell I mentioned at Deal was atrocious, then you should try Beachy Head for a game of nautical marbles!!! Every time the boat plummeted down the well-hole of the sea your stomach stayed behind in mid-air to await the nauseous collision as you rocketed back up to meet it. I'd had enough of being seasick at Deal and I was determined to hang on to my chunda! Anyway, I was now sea secretary, and sea legs were mandatory when you held such an important position. There was no way I was going to lose face in front of the assembled saltwater rabble – no way! The swell was so great that it was difficult to fish the bottom normally and the skipper suggested that we try feathering for mackerel. This we did – and very successfully I might add. You didn't have to jig the feathers, all you needed to do was to hang on to the rod with one hand and the comb hatchings with the other – the swell did the rest! I caught a lot of fish that day; others could have done, but it seems that the weather was getting the better of them. Denny was always seasick so nobody took much notice of him heaving over the side, but when Dibs started to turn green that was a different matter. Chucky, always to joker, knelt in front of his bilious brother and hung two shreds of pork fat from his flaring nostrils. This was too much for Dibs who immediately convulsed and erupted into snot and vomit. Chucky thought this hilarious – but as my mother always said – interminably – God pays debts without money. His turn would come – more sooner than later as it happened. The wind blew, the waves crashed; one minute you were looking down on the ever-descending bows, the next, the stern was towering above your head. Apart from Pancho, Slasher - and me, unbelievably – everybody else was seasick. The decks were littered with groaning zombies. The 'living dead' were athletes compared with our lot! The skipper informed us that the other boat had already gone back to shore to offload the sick and sensitive. He said that we'd also have to go back in so as those that wished too could disembark while the rest of us could go back out with the survivors from the other vessel. Well, I certainly earned my brownie points that day. Let the bad-tempered, loquacious, long-winded committee men fillet the bones out of that – they were all as sick as sea dogs; and I wasn't – SO THERE!!! Some people are so unreasonable. One or two of the committee members – egged on by a mutinous crew no doubt – had the audacity to blame me for the fiasco the day turned out to be for most of the jelly-legged, green-gilled, excuses for seamen – or should I say semen? WANKERS!!! The wind was my fault, the scudding clouds were my fault, the rain was my fault, and even their lily-livered seasickness was my fault! Ungrateful bastards! I'd spent days organizing that trip and didn't even charge expenses. Phone calls, stamps, stationery, not a bean – nothing. I've dealt with committees on and off all my life and it's true to say that those that moan the most about what the committee have done - or not done - are the very last ones to get up off their fat arses and volunteer for anything. Ungrateful bastards!!! But was I put off – not a bit of it. I'd been invested with a certain amount of authority and I was determined to carry out my duties both deftly and diligently for as long as the ill-mannered, barracking circumstances allowed.

The next venue I was asked to book was Ludham Bridge on the River Ant in Norfolk. I contacted the local coach hire firm in Pitsea – Campbells – and arranged times, dates and finances. The morning of the trip duly arrived and we entered the portals of our local hostelry shortly before first-light. Being as I, and most of the assembled crew had only left the selfsame den of depraved iniquity at 11pm the previous evening, none of us really felt up to much. Normally a stickler for teetotal fishing I felt that 'a hair of the dog' was definitely in order. Three pints later and I was ready to sing along with the rest of them. It's surprising what alcohol can do when it comes to healing the festering rifts that occasionally open up in any of life's fractious little fraternities. My one-time angling adversaries were now the most amiable creatures this side of fairyland. But would it last? Would this moratorium of bonhomie that now existed between authority and the masses be sustainable? We would see! Things started off well enough. The coach was smooth and comfortable. The driver friendly and polite - in fact it was the owner of the firm, old Mr. Campbell himself. No, this was going to be a good day, I was sure of it. The sun was as gold as, well - gold! The sky was blue, which was familiar and somewhat comforting, in a blue sort of way! The trees were green, as is their wont – except in autumn of course! And birdsong was birdsong, to add a certain sense of security to the already familiar. What could go wrong? Nothing – surely? When we were well into Norfolk we came to a stop beside a boatyard, some shops, a bridge and a river. "Where's this?" I asked the driver innocently. "Lodden Bridge," he replied, in a somewhat self-satisfied manner. "But we're going to Ludham Bridge," I interjected, forcefully. "You told me Lodden Bridge," he insisted. "No I bloody well didn't!" I confirmed, caustically, "I said Ludham Bridge!" Well, it was no use arguing. My re-established brotherliness with all and sundry looked distinctly as if moratoriums were no longer applicable and to add to that the inordinate length of the River Yare separated us and our angling desires from the official destination – Ludham Bridge!!! Maps were consulted. "We could use the Reedham chain ferry," I said, hopefully. Mr. Campbell, scratched his head, stroked his chin, looked at me askance and then reluctantly agreed. As we got closer to the chain ferry the road – if you could call it a road – started to narrow alarmingly! Eventually we joined a queue of traffic between the flat, reed-lined marshes of the Yare, and waited our turn to cross the waterway. The ferry usually took three cars across at a time and when the ferryman saw our coach there was a look of disbelief on his face that could not have been willingly suspended by the most proficient of playwrights! "Ooooh, I don't be knowing about thaat," he drawled, rustically, "it be a bit big that do." Eventually he was persuaded to give it a go. Mr. Campbell drove the front wheels onto the pontoon and Archimedes' famous law was immediately in evidence. "Jesus Christ!" said one of the assembled, less than reassuringly, "he's going to plunge nose-first in the drink if he's not careful!" Slowly the craft righted itself and Mr. Campbell eased the coach – gingerly – along the length of the pontoon. Crash!!! As the back wheels hit the pontoon it sank a couple of feet into the river and ripped the back bumper off the coach! Mr. Campbell wasn't best pleased – I can assure you. He threatened surcharges, a boycott of the Winged Horse Angling Club, and anything else he could pass through the gap between his steaming labials! Not an auspicious start to a day's fishing you might think – no sir, not at all. The passage of time and more than a few soothing and reconciliatory words did – to a limited extent – calm old Mr. Campbell down, and he agreed to finish the journey. When we finally arrived at Ludham Bridge it was nearly midday and my somewhat lacklustre credibility with the rest of the brotherhood had dimmed to a decidedly dull, matt finish! "Can't you get anything frigging right!" was the general – and yet again ungrateful – consensus. I wasn't going to argue, what was the point, nobody was going to listen; nobody was going to be reasonable. I wandered off on my own, tackled up on a sharp bend by a boatyard and started to concentrate on roach. Roach – the greatest pacifying influence in my life. Roach – serenity personified! A pair of swallowtail butterflies fluttered across my line of vision and I began to relax. This was the life: the Norfolk Broads, windmills and reed-beds, marsh harriers and swans, bream and roach – bream and ROACH!!! I didn't ledger a lot in those days but I decided to use an open ended feeder attached to fairly light tackle and fish the middle track. I couldn't go wrong, the fish started biting straight away, not finicky bites, a couple of slight knocks followed by a definite, slow pull on the rod tip - and I was in! Most of the fish were goers, some well over a pound, and one or two nudging the two pound mark – brilliant!!! I was using maggots and breadcrumb in the feeder and fishing with casters over the top. A local was watching me and suggested that I try worms for a change. He said that although I might catch a few unwanted eels, if there were any two pound plus roach in the vicinity – then worms would have 'em! I've always been grateful for any local knowledge I can get. So I dug myself a few fat, juicy lobworms, and proceeded to follow his advice. I did catch a few eels but fortunately managed to lip hook most of them. I caught roach as well – lots of them. Mostly around the pound mark – more than good enough in itself of course – but I was eager to catch a specimen or two. And I did – by jingo I did: two prime, plump, pink-bellied roach weighing just over two pounds a piece!!! I can smell them now: the crux of everything rivery; a gift from the gods of silts and cabbage-weed. I would fish the broads again as I got older – many times in fact. But that first taste of roach fishing on the River Ant stays in my mind like an eternal memory – as if situated in some fish-haunted, spiritual dimension of the soul. Roach, red fins, river sheep, *gardon,* whatever – just roach, pure, perfect, unadulterated - ROACH!!!

The time had come to hang up my boots as far as being sheriff of the Winged Horse Angling Club was concerned. I'd had just about enough of all the petty quibbling, the rule book, the ungratefulness and the unreasonable demands on my time and my patience. From now on – I thought, mistakenly as it happens – fishing would be more of a solitary affair of the heart. I'd proved by virtue of the roach I caught on the River Ant that I wasn't as 'incomplete' a dangler as everybody else seemed to assume. I would go it alone and etch my name in the annals of big-fished angling history – I would, I really would. Some hopes!!! At about this time Basildon and I had come to a point of mutual antagonism. I didn't like Basildon any more, owing to the way my childhood had been bricked and concreted over, and my erstwhile friends – mostly married by now – didn't, it seemed to me at the time, have much in common with yours truly. What was I to do? It was obvious really. Where had I spent most of my fun time throughout my teenage years? Southend on Sea of course – good old SOUTHEND!!! I went round to Pancho's and told him of my plans and he very kindly offered to move all my stuff and help me to find somewhere to live. I was twenty three years old and happy to be moving to pastures new. Before long I would find new friends – hopefully angling friends – and life would be all roach and roker once again – plus a few pints of lager of course! Put on your shades and your kiss-me-quick hats and follow me on to the flounder-full shores of the greatest estuary in the universe – probably!!!

Reedham Norfolk - looking towards the ferry

Pitsea marina

Into a big'un

Massive haul of mackerel at Deal
Left to right - Pancho, the author, Slasher and the skipper

Thames barges - Maldon

St Peters-on-the-Wall - Bradwell-juxta-Mare

The saltings - Bradwell Waterside

The British Empire - Battlesbridge - River Crouch

Overtones of the Arctic - winter Battlesbridge

Lion wharf - Creeksea - River Crouch

Mostly mallard - Dedham Mill Pool

Cockle boats at Leigh - January 1987

Jigging for mackerel - Southend Pier

Skate for supper

Holehaven - Canvey Island looking towards the Fobbing Horse

Hadleigh Ray from Two Tree Island - Leigh-on-Sea - Essex

CHAPTER NINE

NEW FRIENDS – SAME WATERS

My fishing did actually start as a solitary pursuit when I first moved to Southend. I was living in a flat in Westcliff, close to the seafront and the then Westcliff Jetty. I liked to fish a summer tide that reached high water between about midnight and three in the morning. That was not only the time for flounders and eels but also perfect for the shore-hugging shoals of school bass – interesting, what! Ragworm and lugworm were good – but as always, crab was even better. On one particular summer morning at about 2am I was walking down to the jetty with my rod over my shoulder and a fishing bag slung from the tip when a policeman on foot patrol eyed me suspiciously from the other side of the road and began to address me sternly. "Where do you think your going at this time in the morning?" To me it was pretty obvious and quick as a flash without even thinking of the consequences I said "Elephant shooting!" "No need to be like that," he replied, disconsolately, "I only wanted a chat, it's lonely out here." And chat we did – so much so that I nearly missed the tide! It turned out that he was an angler himself – both sea and freshwater. Well, you know what it's like once you start talking about fishing – don't you? Garrulousness doesn't come into it, we gabbled away like a couple of old fish wives about every piscatorial subject under the moon. He was a mine of useful information. I thought I already knew quite a lot about the area but he told me things about fish, tackle and tactics, that have since held me in very good stead – very good stead indeed! Please excuse the grammar - I'm a poet you know! Let's get back to Westcliff Jetty. It was a brilliant jetty; fifteen foot high approximately, with a timbered walkway and adjoining platform, railings and wooden stairs, and a lower platform for landing and putting out to sea in a boat. On that specific moonlit night it was warm and calm – dead calm. There were none of the autumn and winter sounds of waders and wildfowl to disturb the silence – a silence that was almost tangible. I tackled up with a running ledger and a single hook, large enough to accommodate a whole crab, and cast in. It wasn't in the water more than a few seconds when the rod snatched violently. It was a school bass of about three quarters of a pound. Greedy little buggers they are – a whole crab; a fortune even in those days if you couldn't find enough of your own to fish with. But who cares? I was fishing and the fish were feeding in return. That jetty was something of a social club really. Tribes of lost and lonely souls, single, or out of favour with their wives, would huddle together for fish and sympathy in every season of the year. I've met some lovely people on that jetty. For all I said to the detriment of anglers in the preceding chapter it has to be said in retrospect that I didn't really mean it – not wholeheartedly that is. Anglers in general – if not always in particular – are the most genial of fellows – and lasses of course. There's something about fishing that breeds manners, harmony and tolerance. Perhaps it's that indefinable sense of everybody operating with a single purpose in mind? I don't know? But like the lonely, late night policeman when one angler meets another there's an immediate, palpable rush, of arterial camaraderie – don't you think? No, don't worry, I'm not going to break the spell by relating some dastardly deed perpetrated against my person by another practitioner of this sacred art of ours. No, in general I like most anglers, and although I've spent a lot of time fishing on my own I'm more than happy to chat with a fellow dangler and to share my bait or my limited knowledge. Although, as I've said, the jetty was mostly only good for flounders and eels – with the occasional school of summer bass; the sport could become fast and furious in winter with some reasonable whiting. All you needed was a high tide and a stiff onshore wind and you were in with a chance of filling the freezer! Difficult fishing conditions of course, but when did that ever stop the dedicated among us? No, Westcliff Jetty was okay, even in the daytime you could pick up a few good eels and flatties – well worth the effort, I think.

It was time to try my luck on Southend Pier again. I already knew most of the best spots and what species of fish I was likely to catch from them. But one is not always prepared for every eventuality – is one? On one glorious summer's day, with the sun reflecting and refracting off the sparkling, silver water, and the gulls breasting the incoming breeze with their dazzling plumage, I decided to fish by the station. I was fishing with lugworm, and following a more 'chuck it and chance it' procedure than I would normally. On either side of me anglers were fishing up in the water, either with a boom or a float, and catching the occasional garfish. I wasn't keen on them myself; something about their green flesh didn't suit my temperament or my taste buds for that matter. So I wasn't really bothered. Then the gulls started to congregate overhead as a large shoal of mackerel came our way. Immediately those fishing up in the water started to catch. Fishing for garfish they were using slithers of silver herring which suited the mackerel very well. Other anglers immediately put on feathers and joined in with the action. All I had was lugworm on the bottom and they certainly weren't interested in that! Improvisation was needed – what could I do? In those days I smoked Players Number Six. I put a boom on my line that would hold position at about four feet under the surface, tied a small long-shanked hook to a short trace, and fixed it to the boom. And then the *piece de resistance* – silver paper from my cigarette packet wrapped around the hook! It worked a treat, in no time at all I was pulling them in as fast as everyone else. Who says that it doesn't pay to read Edward De Bono? Lateral thinking, that's all it takes - lateral thinking! After so many fires – both at the pier head and the shore end – it has to be said that it's pretty pathetic nowadays as compared with its former glory. There have been at different times, roller skating rinks and bowling alleys near the entrance to the pier, and more fun than you could shake a stick at, at the seaward end. Apart from the normal amusement arcades there was a sundeck, a cafeteria, a theatre, a seawater aquarium and much, much more. To fish on East Point for dabs until hungry and thirsty, and then to tie your rod up and repair to the cafeteria for a hot steak and kidney pie with lashings of thick brown gravy, followed by a steaming mug-full of equally hot sweet tea, had a salt taste and a sea-refreshing tang about it that I can still savour to this very day! Smells, we don't think about them much; but just writing this I can smell the very estuary itself. Bladderwrack and burgers, timber and tackle shops, slipways and seaweed, I can smell them all as they permeate the recesses of my subconscious imagining mind. Time has all but disappeared. I'm there, and it's then. Now is then and then is now, time is meaningless. I'm like a Bisto Kid at the whiff of such nostalgia. Is it the 50's or the 90's, what's the difference? The sea is eternal and so are we. Breathe deep my friends, breathe deep. The tide turns, it ebbs and it flows, always has, always will. What goes returns, what dies will live again. Who said that fishermen think of nothing except fish? Water my friends, the emotional, spiritual, and physical depths of our very being. The great subconscious tides of our collective existence. All is one my friends, as above so below. No-one was born so no-one can die, we were always here and we always will be – you can see it in the eye of a fish my friends as well as in a grain of sand from the beach. Fear not, you will fish forever – you are the fish and the fish is you; believe me my friends, it's true. What was I saying about bladderwrack? I seem to have lost the line somewhere along the way – excuse me, my patient exponents of the trusty rod and angle; I have these funny turns occasionally, it will pass I can assure you, it usually does!

My solitary fishing expedition's were about to come to an end. I'd met a new friend in the pub – John Anson – and what's more he had a boat: a beautiful little 18ft, two-berth, fibreglass Shetland. Apart from the cabin with its cooking facilities, the covered cockpit, and the two 16 horse Evenrudes attached to the transom. It had the attention of two eager anglers desperate to use it to its full potential! We went everywhere in that boat; from Canvey Point to the South East Maplin – and beyond. When you turned on the power you could get to the Maplins and back in half the time it took most of the other charter boats. For me it was 'a dream come true'. Boat fishing whenever I wanted it; all I had to do was dig some bait and pay for my share of the petrol – stupendous!!! John was one of the nicest men you could ever wish to meet. A gentle, amiable soul, who would do anything for anyone – he was a gem. And a damn good angler to boot! I've fished from that boat in just about every type of weather imaginable. I've come into the mooring late at night in a January blizzard with the visibility so poor that you couldn't even see the lights along the shoreline! I've fished when waves have turned to ice immediately they came into contact with the deck! I've sat out on the mooring under the stars with frost on my beard and icicles forming on the end of my nose! In summer it's been so hot at times that paint began to blister on the woodwork and the bilges took on the olfactory similitude of a rancid, festering bouillabaisse. I've caught bass – not by the hundredweight admittedly – but enough to keep my own fish soup bubbling away from one end of the summer to the other. I've caught eels as thick as my limitless imagination and stewed and jellied them until the fridge started to buckle and my belly began to follow suit! Happy days – ah, happy days!!! Whether it was the Chapman Sands, the Low Way, the Middle Grounds, any of the Shoebury Buoys or out to the South East Maplin and beyond, fishing, whether fast and furious or slack and unprofitable, was our *raison d'etre*. We would fish until we dropped. We were insatiable in the face of the deeps and the swatchways, the channels and the shoal waters, the bars and the gullies and the sandbanks. Fishing, fishing, fishing – what else was life for? I remember one hot summer's day motoring out at full speed ahead to the South East Maplin to fish a double tide. We had no particular species in mind: bass, skate, dogfish, it didn't matter. We were fishing – and that was enough. The sea was like chromium plate: a shimmering, quick-silvered, sun-glancing, dazzle of a day. The sky was a hazy, cerulean blue, and the sun's doubloon defied the eyes with its gold-coined intensity. Cormorants sank into the mercurial waters like submarines and surfaced again with flounders in their bills. Little terns hovered and dived in the swatchways and black-headed gulls screeched as if rending the sea's own precious metals. It was perfect – absolutely perfect! As the tide fell we found ourselves in one of the low water gullies surrounded by sandbanks and the gentle slap and susurration of the waves. The tide was slack but there was still more than enough water to fish in. We were fishing with our normal running ledgers, six foot traces, and fairly large hooks in the hopes of catching a bass or a skate. I was using strips of herring for bait and casting out about twenty feet from the boat. We didn't get either bass or skate on that particular day –

unfortunately. But what we did get were spurdog – baby spurdog; hundreds of them. I don't know whether or not you've ever handled eight inch baby spurdog – but they're wriggly little bastards; and that's saying something! What's more – in compliance with their name – they have sharp little spurs along their backs that can inflict quite a nasty wound. Small perhaps, but painful nevertheless! My hands were covered in them. Pinpricks almost, blue in the centre, shading to purple and red as the inflammation spread out across the skin. Not the greatest of fun I have to say. It seems that the most perfect of days can still be spoilt by unexpected occurrences! I'd never caught baby spurdog before and I've never caught them since. No synchronicity there then!!! What next – let me think? Mmmmmmmmm! Eels, not everybody's 'kettle of fish' that's for sure, but I've always had a soft spot for them – mostly close to the lining of the stomach it has to be admitted! In the summer of 76 – sounds almost American that – doesn't it?   - We caught eels the like we'd never caught before. If you're old enough to remember, that was one of the longest and hottest summers on record. The water temperature in the Estuary was degrees higher than normal and the eels were not only more prolific but much larger than the usual run of things. Two pound eels were commonplace right through from August until the beginning of November! Most of our large hauls came straight off of the mooring – there was no need to start the engines; there were eels everywhere. Thinking about it, I bet none of those holidaymakers frolicking in those sub tropical waters were aware of their unwanted guests! Imagine getting a two pound eel up one of your unprotected orifices –

it doesn't bear thinking about does it!!! It wasn't all sunshine and roses in those days – I don't suppose that it ever was really. There was a lot of pilferage going on at night when the tide was out. You daren't leave your outboards attached when you finished fishing because the chances were that they'd be gone by the next day. I had a bad hip and it was getting worse year by year, so I found trudging through the ooze with a 16 horse Evenrude on my shoulder something of an unwanted encumbrance. Not only did we have to shift the outboards but then we had to go back and collect our fishing tackle - and fish if we'd caught any! After one particularly exhausting day, fishing a double tide, John decided to take a chance and padlock the outboards in the cabin. The gods seemed to be with us, we left them there for weeks and every time we went to fish – there they were, completely unmolested. Another of our friends – a non-angler it has to be said – felt as though he'd like to try his luck at the piscatorial arts and asked John if he could fish all night from the mooring. John being the genial, amiable, personage already described, willingly obliged. It transpires that at some time during the night the non-angler in question somehow managed to smash one of the six inch side windows situated at the top of the cabin. He didn't think to do anything about it – who would if they were a stranger to the ways of the sea? When he'd finished fishing he locked up and fastened John's green tarpaulin over the roof. Unfortunately, he didn't fasten the tarpaulin tightly to the cleats, and consequently left a loop of lose material hanging down below the gunnels. This of course – spelt disaster! The tide returned, seawater got into the loop, tilted the boat to starboard, and spilled through

the broken window into the cabin. It sunk of course –
what else could it do? So although nobody had stolen
the outboards since we'd left them in the cabin, the sea
had done something equally as disheartening. You
should have seen the state of that boat! When we had
bailed out the water there was still six inches of
stinking silt to contend with. The engines were ruined
– at least that's what I thought. We managed to clean
the boat up, fixed the window, waited for the tide to
come in and left it to its own devices. "I'm sorry
Merv." Said John, apologetically, "but I'm afraid
we're going to have to carry these outboards back to
shore again." "What are you going to do with them," I
said curiously, "scrap them?" "You must be joking,"
he replied, in an uncharacteristically sharp manner," "I
didn't do a five year apprenticeship in the motor trade
for nothing; I'll fix the bastards if it kills me!" And it
probably would I thought – probably would! But true
to his word the next time I saw him they were once
again attached to the transom and purring like
contented moggies. We didn't always go boat fishing.
John did a lot of work on the power stations in Kent
and knew his way around the best shore-fishing spots.
I can't remember which power station it was now
exactly but I think it was on the Isle of Grain.
Whatever, John told me that you could catch good bass
there in the winter! Migratory fish in the winter I
thought, he must be kidding – but he wasn't! The
warm water outflow from that particular power station
flowed out into a long creek and the bass were more
than happy to stay there all winter basking in the tepid
waters! To get there you had to climb a barbed wire
fence and trespass across a mile of bushy scrub and

grass cropped close by the thousands of rampaging rabbits. There seemed to be a goodly mixture of wild, semi wild and domesticated coneys. Some were even jet black! But enough of the rabbit pie, let's get back to the bass. The best way to catch them was by spinning. I used a very light spinning rod, a freshwater reel and the smallest silver spinner I owned. Sink and draw was the method – and it was a killer! They only ranged between a pound and three pound in weight but it was brilliant sport. We went week in week out. I fished there once when large, goose-feathered flakes of snow were tumbling erratically down out of a cold and leaden January sky. To catch bass in the snow is somewhat incongruous to say the least. Like floating crust for carp in the Arctic Ocean!!! But it was unbelievably exciting, bass on light spinning gear fight like crazy, and the take when they grab the spinner – well, it nearly jolts your arm out of its sockets! Further down the creek there was a bridge and beyond that the creek widened out and deepened. Once the news got around it was like the Spanish Armada down there – there were small boats everywhere! Unfortunately this had the effect of alerting the powers that be to the trespassers in their midst and before long the authorities put a ban on fishing in that particular creek. But it was great fun while it lasted. We could see those fishing from small boats in the deeper water pulling far bigger bass than we'd caught over the side, and I'm sure if it wasn't for the inevitable ban John and I would have motored over there from Southend and taken our share of the action. Never mind, we enjoyed the time we had, and how many people do you know who have filled their creels with bass in a snowstorm?

Sometimes for a change of scenery we'd charter a boat elsewhere. One of our favourite spots was Southwold on the Suffolk coast. You picked up the boat in a tidal river near the town, motored down to the harbour to negotiate the ever-shifting sands and shingle in the harbour mouth, and then travelled out of sight of land far into the grey, unending vistas of the cold North Sea. We drove up there one February in the frost – hoping for some big cod. It was a bitterly cold day. We were wearing so much clothing by to time we got onboard that we looked like a couple of Michelin Men!!! There had been a storm a few days before and although it was calm on that particular day the after effects were felt in the form of a very heavy swell. And you know how I feel about swells – don't you? We never had a knock all day. The boatman – sporting a blue nose and even bluer fingers – suggested that we might like to go back in. We were having none of it, we'd paid our money and we were going to damn well make the most of it! It got colder and colder. I couldn't feel anything; which was very fortunate, because if I could have, whatever it was would have probably felt very painful indeed!!! As the saltwater sprayed over the gunnels it started to freeze on the decks. The boatman was looking at us with sea hooks for eyes – he was frozen to the core. But would we give in? Would we buggery! A seal popped up in front of us and twitched his curious whiskers. If we could have read his subaqueous mind we'd have probably been extremely embarrassed. I've got to be here, he'd probably be thinking, I live here – but as for these two-legged pratts, well, they must be stark raving bonkers! We did eventually concede fishless defeat but not until the sun was red, rounded, and recumbent in the west, and our toes were like frozen shrimps; wriggle-less in our less than thermal boots! The journey home was all teeth chatter and chilblains and the frost was as thick as new fallen snow on the roadside verges. As I said earlier, I'm more of a fair weather fisherman now that I'm older. I do still fish in the winter on milder days but I'd never do another trip like that one to Southwold – not in a million years – Never!!!

I fished with John Anson on his boat for quite a few years – and great years they were too. We didn't only sea fish, John belonged to a freshwater angling club that had waters in Hanningfield in Essex and could occasionally get me a guest ticket. It was a lake the club had dug for themselves – not such a common practice in those days – and it was well stocked with carp, tench, roach, rudd and bream. They had their own hut with cooking facilities, a toilet and some bunks – quite the proto-commercial carp puddle really! I fished there with John all night on numerous occasions and the fish were quite often obliging. We were fairly close to a decent pub and equally as often we'd walk along the field borders under the owl-hooting moon to sample a pint or two of angler's 'old reserve' – cheers! Ah, that's better!!! There's something very special about a pub when you're fishing: the banter, the tall tales, the bonhomie, and everything else that goes with pints and piscatorial reminiscences – marvellous! I've also fished with John and his wife on boating holidays on the Norfolk Broads – but more of that later. At about this time I met two other people in the same pub where I'd met John – Morty – a middle-aged Scotsman from the hills just west of Aberdeen, and Colin, a young man of about my own age. It turned out that they were both anglers as well. Primarily coarse fishermen but not averse to a quick dabble in the briny when the fancy took them! We too became good friends and it wasn't long before the conversation turned to the possibility of us all going freshwater fishing together. There were mostly day ticket waters in our particular area in those days and quite often when you got to the bank all the best swims were already occupied. We decided to join a club and there was one based not that far from us that managed about a dozen lakes and as many miles of river in various parts of Essex. Join, we duly did, and the next chapter is about – amongst other fishing related subjects – the tentative first steps to becoming a fully proficient club angler, or something like that! You're well aware of the trouble I had with the one and only other club I'd been a member of – let's hope the new experience will turn out to be a more pleasurable and profitable one! Let's hope!!!

CHAPTER TEN

THE BILLERICAY AND DISTRICT
ANGLING CLUB

We joined the BDAC in 1976 and for those of you that
remember it was to longest, hottest and driest summer
on record. Early on in the season we regularly fished
one of the club's three freehold waters – Southminster
Lakes. They were old gravel workings situated to the
east of the town itself and they overlooked the farms
and the marshes that stretched their lonely, desolate
miles, all the way to the edge of the grey North Sea.
The lakes themselves were far from desolate; the club
had worked wonders with them. Apart from stocking,
swim building and general maintenance, they'd also
instigated a conservation policy. Indigenous trees and
shrubs had been planted and by the time we arrived
they were already reaching maturity. The lakes were
looking very natural indeed. The club even went as far
as giving advice on the protection of wildlife in their
handbook. Bird calls and alarms were to be taken
seriously, and if any of our feathered friends seemed
particularly agitated, it was suggested that we moved
swims just in case we were disturbing a nest site!
Forward thinking indeed – I'd say! Due to the
exceptional weather that summer there was
unfortunately a certain amount of fish loss. The culprit
– as nearly always – was deoxygenation and pumps
were duly installed to alleviate the problem. Another
strange thing that we observed first hand was how fish
grow to the size of the water they live in – excepting of

course with the feeding regimes on commercials nowadays! Perhaps I shouldn't have said grow – in this particular case the correct terminology would have been – shrink!!! They'd stocked one of the lakes with a number of ten pound bream from Abberton Reservoir near Colchester. Within a year or so half of them had died and the remainder had shrunk down to about five pounds a piece! Mind you, those that were left were very healthy specimens and I'm sure if it hadn't have been for the exceptionally hot weather in '75' and '76' most of the others would have survived as well. There were about nine lakes at the Southminster complex and over a period of months we managed to fish all of them – except the trout lake that is! Morty had an old 30cwt Commer van and we usually went on a Friday night and stayed right through until Sunday evening. Tilly Lamps, a gas burner and sleeping bags, were all we needed by the way of creature comforts, and some of my happiest memories revolve around those magical weekends. Morty – God bless him – had very poor eyesight and spent much of the time with spectacles perched on the end of his nose, with his tongue stuck out in concentration, trying to thread very fine nylon monofilament through the eyes of hooks! Being of Highland sheep farming stock he was more used to the fly than baits and coarse fishing, but had adapted well and caught more than his fair share of fish. Colin was another of those born anglers we've all come across from time to time. He could sense fish in his swim – it was almost primal – the archetypical hunter's instinct. In the two years that we belonged to the club, he was the first to catch one of those five pound bream – and the last!!! He usually caught a better stamp of fish than me or Morty – but we had our moments. One of my favourite lakes was one of the smallest. Stocks seemed to consist mainly of rudd – there were thousands of them! Not all tiddlers either, many of them were of a very respectable size – 6 to 12ozs. A few were much bigger! If I wanted to get into the better specimens I'd wait until evening and fish until it got dark. Maggots were as good a bait as any, the smaller fish seemed to feed during the heat of the day and the larger ones came on song in the evening. Spraying maggots and fishing shirt button style on the drop was the best method. When they really started to feed you'd get a fish a cast – and some really good fish at that. If the bait found its way to the bottom unmolested and you were prepared to forgo the pleasure of rudd fishing for a while, then a tench or two would invariably pick up your hook bait and head off for the reeds at a furious pace! Not massive tench, perhaps only a pound or two, but very exciting in a confined space surrounded by reed beds and overhanging bushes. The little tincas!!! Some of those summer evenings were unforgettable: warm, not a breath of air, the moon changing shifts with the sun, and the tawny owls - tu-whit-tu-wooing - and exchanging hoots as only owls know how. Sometimes, if there was an exceptional hatch of midges, the swallows and swifts would arrive out of seemingly nowhere in their hundreds and thousands. Veritable clouds of those avian acrobats cart-wheeling across the water's surface and shattering the satin sheen of the moon's last-light meniscus – unbelievable!!! As the midges rose – so would they. The black swifts, curved and cuneiform, like some ancient and indecipherable language, went on and up into the farthest reaches of the darkening sky to fly all night under the leaching light emitted from the oh so far and scintillating stars. The swallows, blue-black and white, like a mixture of snow and tempered steel, twittered from their brick-dusted throats then disappeared as quickly as they came to roost in the shadows of the silken hedgerows. I've just got to mention Jack Hargreaves again – 'the angler's other eye' – that's what it's all about – surely!!!

As previously mentioned, for my part pubs and angling go together. Southminster was no exception to that particularly infallible rule! The Railway Tavern was just a few dry mouthwatering yards from the fish and their own unquenchable waterholes – Do fish drink, by the way? I've never thought about it before! Anyway, forget that; let's get back to the pub. The Railway was a traditional inn. Good beer, hot steak and kidney pies, and buxom barmaids – very buxom indeed! One of the barmaids was so buxom in fact that if she stood by the window the moonlight was immediately eclipsed! That wench to out-wench all wenches seemed to fancy me. Well, it has to be said that although I was never that fussy – I couldn't afford to be considering my mirrors cracked and impartial opinion – but I did have a bad hip and mountain climbing was definitely not my forte! Some of the looks she gave me would have shrivelled the testes of an elephant! As far as she was concerned my erogenous zones might just have well have been on the other side of Alpha Centauri – she could keep her salivating love-bites to herself!!! My friends – as is the ever-ambivalent way with interpersonal relationships – thought it was hilarious. So much so that whenever I went to point Percy to porcelain they would sidle up to her at the bar and tell her just how much I fancied her! He's just shy, they would say, that's all, just shy. Well, that gigantic broad gave me the sort of coy, simpering glances that would have been capable of souring a dozen firkins of the finest best bitter - I was terrified!!! There was only one thing for it – "take no notice of my friends," I said, in a whispered and confidential way, "they're just winding you up – I'm GAY!!!" This did the trick, she turned almost instantly from a lusting, lascivious vamp, into to a motherly – not to say almost smotherly – concerned and caring confidant. The only trouble being that I didn't know that she was also the local blabber mouth! Subsequent to that particular occasion, every time I went into the pub, all the gnarled, big-fisted, sons of the surrounding soil, gave me looks that were just as withering – if not more so – than the ones I'd originally received from the ever-bourgeoning Earth Mother herself. Prejudice, sexism, fatism, homophobia, you just can't win – honestly; it's impossible!

After the pub there were the regulation bacon sandwiches, mugs of hot tea, and a few hours fitful, fart permeated, noxious sleep, before first-light crept up warmly and slowly from the shores of the ever-present, whispering northern sea. Dawn and angling – what compatible fellows they are – if you'll excuse the anthropomorphism, that is! Lily pads and low light; birdsong and bat-flittering aerobatics, fish leaps and far fathoming concentricity – what more could a man want – or a woman for that matter? Fishing at dusk is great, but unfortunately, as is the diurnal way of things, it eventually gets dark! Fishing at dawn, well, that's different. The curve of the earth can do nothing but turn towards the east and reveal the red, distended disk of the sun – it's inevitable; at least, I hope so!!! Eighteen hours of solid fishing if you have the stamina – the Lord be praised! No, fishing at dawn just after first-light, when the water's as still as infinity and the float twitches and dips in the shimmering silks of the lake's dusky – yet sometimes – rippled and sun-quickening, opalescent surface; that's the place to be – there's nowhere else like it! Nowhere in the whole of God's endless and unfathomable universe – nowhere!!! I saw a boy on one of those lakes, fishing with his father, and using a match rod with 3lb line and a 16 hook, strike into a 15lb common carp – and land it! It took at least thirty minutes, but you've got to give him his due, he got it into the landing net – on his own! Miracles do happen occasionally my friends – they do, believe me – especially at dawn in the middle of a glorious summer – they really do! I've never caught a carp as big as that, but then I've never really fished for them. I was not jealous in the slightest; in fact I was pleased for the lad, and probably nearly enjoyed the experience as much as he did. But occasionally I do suffer from a smidgen of green-eyed malevolence. The largest tench I've ever caught was five pounds in weight. That fish took me years of study to catch. I've read more words about tench than a cartload of fishery officers; have paid more attention to watercraft than your average otter. And what did I hear on one of those lakes from the lips of a mere strippling? I'll tell you what I heard! He was fishing specifically for carp; nothing else mind you – all tautology aside that is – when he struck into a good run. And what did he catch? I'll tell you what he caught – a 6lb tench, that's what!!! And what's worse, he spoke about it with such an air of carp-denied disappointment that I could have strangled the little git – then and there!!! It's a good job I've never had children, that's all I can say! A bloody good job!!!

Another of the BDAC's waters – Straits Mill – at Braintree was also well worth a visit. Every year tench over 8lb's were regularly caught and in those day they were considered monsters. Both rudd and roach reached specimen sizes and double figure carp and pike were also present. Along the southern edge of the lake one of the sections of the freshwater River Blackwater wound its glorious, reed whispering way beneath willows and alders. That particular stretch was also managed by the BDAC and was a very good fishery for chub and roach – especially in winter when it had a bit of colour. We regularly fished the lake in the summer of '76' – that really does sound American – doesn't it? By August that year's drought was at its worst. Some of the underwater features of the ex gravel working were beginning to show themselves: gravel bars, gullies, deeps, shallows and sandbanks. If ever there was a lesson to show the merits of carefully plumbing a water before fishing, it was there to be seen before one's very eyes! I decided to float fish from a newly arisen sandbank into reasonably clear yet deepish water. As I threw in a handful of maggots I could see the silver and gold sides of roach and rudd as they turned to take the feed. It was like some form of piscatorial semaphore – and I certainly got the message! I decided to fish fairly light with 2lb line straight through and a size 16 hook. Normally maggots pick up predominantly small fry but on this occasion the stamp of fish was definitely better than average. Plenty of rudd and roach between three quarters of a pound and a pound and a quarter found their way into my busy landing net. I've already told you what I think about roach and it has to be said that I find rudd almost equally endearing. Small rudd are beautiful enough but as they increase in size their scales become more deeply golden and their fins take on the sheen of rubies. To catch rudd like those in a lake is like opening a treasure chest! Nay, precious stones and metals are as nothing when compared with those dazzling denizens of the deeps – they're incomparable! Colin was fishing close into the margins under an overhanging tree and the stamp of his fish – as usual – was even better than mine. He caught a number of stupendous roach and rudd teetering on the 2lb mark! I wasn't envious though, a 2lb roach would have gone down well of course, but I was more than contented with the results of my fine line and light tackle tactics. In the summer if the fish weren't biting you could always have a picnic by the river. The green, blue and red metallic sheen of demoiselles fluttered in and out of the reeds and rushes and made all the tales of angels and fairies seem almost believable. Kingfishers sped back and forth along the river like sapphire skies and orange sunsets, and swans, with the softest and whitest of raised wings you've ever seen, sailed like galleons on the whispering summer breezes – it was perfect!

We didn't always fish the club's lakes; sometimes we made an excursion to one of their many stretches of river. Blue Mills on the River Blackwater near Witham was a favoured location. Much of the river was shallow, quite fast, and difficult to fish. If you were prepared to walk some distance in a westerly direction you could find some deep holes under the trees that were perfect for tempting a decent chub or two. If you wanted to fish the faster, shallower water, stret-pegging and ledgering were probably the best methods, but we preferred to fish further east where a bend run up against some wooden pilings. There you could catch a nice mixed bag of dace, roach, perch, and the occasional chub, by fishing close to the piles from the other side of the relatively narrow river. It wasn't easy, especially in the wind or when the river was fining down after a spate but still faster than usual, but it was well worth the effort involved! I've had some lovely bags of fish from that particular stretch of river, plenty of goers, with the perch especially coming up trumps as far as size was concerned. Another river the club managed was the Pant. The Pant is actually the same river as the Blackwater! The name is dependent on which side of Braintree you are fishing – east or west. The Pant was a very prolific little river – and still is! In those days, as well as the normal chub, roach, dace and perch, you could also be pleasantly surprised by the occasional brown trout or grayling – very up market, what!!! What I loved most about the river was the large head of dace that it held – beautiful, large, powerful, streamlined silver dace. You could stand by any of the fords that crossed the narrow country lanes and see massive shoals of them, head against the current waiting for any morsels that happened to come their way. I love dace fishing – the lunge, shake, splash and the fury of it! You could catch them with a bubble float, freelining, or with a fly rod if you fancied donning your tweeds and gaiters!!! Dace of a half a pound were not uncommon and there were some that nudged the pound mark! Casters, bread – flake or punch – and maggots were all good baits on their day. In summer you would find them in the shallow glides but in winter the bigger fish would go deeper and you'd often find them in the same places as the chub. I've heard tales of chub touching 6lb being caught from this tiny river but the best I ever managed was about 3lb. The club also had stretches of the River Roding between Ongar and Aybridge but we never fished those in the two years that we were in the club so all I can say about them is that according to other members that had they were also excellent for chub and roach fishing – especially in winter when the weed growth had died back. A simple arlesey bomb with bread flake being the killer tactic!

Great Totham, between Maldon and Tiptree, was another place that received more than its fair share of our attention. There were two lakes, one either side of a country road. One was something of a specimen lake, hard fishing, but the place to go if you were a carp man. The other – that we fished, naturally – was a lot easier. It was a small ex gravel working with unbelievably steep sides – almost precipitous in fact! But once you got down there – twenty feet beneath the surrounding countryside you were well protected from the wind. Even in a gale the surface could be as calm as the proverbial mill pond! It was something of a mixed fishery – the ideal place for 'pleasure anglers' in fact. But we weren't there for pleasure we had our eye on its large stock of crucian carp! They were best fished for in the summer months with dawn and dusk being the best times – very crepuscular!!! I remember one particular day in July. It was as hot as cinders and there was not a breath of air. All was silence except for the monotonous trill and wheeze of the yellowhammers and the lovelorn accompaniment of stridulating grasshoppers and crickets. Cabbage-white butterflies fluttered haphazardly; came together in pairs, spiralled into the air in territorial convolutions and then separated only to flutter off again into their solo, aerial balletics. It was so hot that nothing was feeding – except for the ducks; God bless 'em!!! As the day started to cool and the light began to lower we started to get the first finicky and infuriating bites shy crucians are so famed for. If you caught one in ten you considered yourself lucky! Slowly but surely – loose feeding hemp and sweetcorn little and often – the takes became more positive. By the time the sun had started to set the fish were as confident as concubines and the sport became very hectic. They were good crucians too ranging from between one and two pounds – with the occasional one even larger! Golden muscled; compact, rounded and powerful – fantastic fishing!!! I was fishing with both bread flake and sweetcorn and by this

time I'd attracted quite a few little 'friends' - RATS –
as bold as bollocks and twice as nasty - or so most
people would tell you. Quite honesty, I found them
rather sweet – weil's disease aside that is!!! Between
feeding the fish and wetting the lading net, I started to
feed them. They actually came right up to me and took
the bread out of my hand! They sat on their haunches
with the pieces of bread clutched in their tiny paws and
nibbled away like squirrels with their whiskers
continually twitching – enchanting – don't you think?
Okay, I wouldn't want a cartload of them stuffed
inside my trousers, but I do think they get something
of a bad press. They're tolerated in children's books –
'The Wind in the Willows' for example – and white,
tame rats are considered as fluffy and lovable as kittens
and puppies; but whenever a wild one is seen in
suburbia or around the farm – BINGO!!! Out come the
Jack Russells and the ferrets, poisons are mixed, guns
loaded, and screams and curses issued! Poor little furry
creatures – is it their fault that we leave so much
garbage around that they're in danger of exponential
distension? I told you I was a smart arse – didn't I! No,
I'm joining the 'League against Cruelty to Rodents' –
forthwith! Join me brothers – stuff the antis; who do
they think they are? As the evening drew on and the
moon lifted its amber weight above the summer
horizon and the first few stars twinkled and iridesced
in the sky and the silken waters, the float became
harder and harder to see, but I was so obsessed I just
couldn't think of stopping fishing – no way! I had a
small torch and I shone its pin point, diminutive beam
onto the darkening float. The fish just wouldn't stop
coming. The golden scales and moon-silvered water

thrashed in a spray of electrifying crystals – it was breathtaking! We had to finish eventually – we weren't supposed to be fishing there at night anyway! I could hardly lift my keepnet out of the water it was so heavy – yes, we bagged up even in those far off days! Colin and Morty and me, said goodbye to the rats, the moon and the starlit sky and made our way the nearest hostelry for repartee and liquid refreshment – game over!!! There's just one more BDAC lake that I'd like to mention – Asheldam. Situated between Tillingham and Southminster on the Dengie Peninsula it was the epitome of the traditional, natural water. Although an old gravel-working it had matured to such an extent that you would have been hard put to ascertain its former function – it was perfect. It was steep sided with overhanging willows and alders. It had so many small and large bays that there was not one swim on the entire lake that you could see all the others from! Lily pads, rushes, reeds, birdsong and bucolic reveries – what more could an angler want? It contained excellent carp, specimen roach, rudd and perch, and a few indigenous, long-time resident tench. It was fished mostly for its head of good carp but being a 'roach man' they didn't concern me much. Hemp and wheat in the shallows in summer and worm and maggots in the deeps in the winter – that was my approach. Did you notice that the word 'approach' is an acronym for 'A Perfect, Prime, ROACH'? Synchronicity, you see; I've told you before, it's fate my friends – FATE!!! We caught some lovely roach at Asheldam. Being as most everybody else was fishing for carp the roach weren't as wary as the might otherwise have been – very fortunate for 'The Incomplete Dangler" – I'd say!

We didn't just fish BDAC waters at that time. We still made regular visits to my favourite River Chelmer and had some good catches to prove it! In the summer wheat was my preferred bait for roach fishing. Between Paper Mills and Rushes Lock there were a lot of long reaches between the bends. We used to like to fish from the tow path looking across to a line of chattering poplars. On summer afternoons when not much was happening if you fished up in the water along the wind-rippled, sun-sparkling, middle track, you were sure to pick up roach – with a few decent fish amongst them. I've spent many a happy afternoon just waiting for the float to stop momentarily or to dip imperceptibly – that was enough; all the indication you need to strike. It was wonderful fishing and now I've started to use the pole for the first time in my life there's not doubt that I'll be giving it another go – and SOON!!! Close to the reach in question there was a wide bend with deep water close in to the bank. This was where we fished for perch, tench and bream. They say that everything comes in threes! Well, on one particular day I proved the maxim to be correct. I was laying-on with a worm in deep slack water when the float slid away like it was looking for Australia! I struck, and immediately knew I was into a good fish. It fought deep and hard and being as I was using relatively light tackle – 3lb main line and a 2lb hook length; as you do on canals – it was quite some time before I saw the beast. I suspected that it was a tench and I was eventually proved to be correct. Well over 4lb's of deep, olive-tinted magnificence slowly but surely tired enough for me to lift its head and draw it across the waiting net. Number one of the three – not a bad start, not a bad start at all! I replenished the ground bait, put another worm on the hook, and cast into the same spot. In no time at all the float sailed away again. I struck, and I was into another furious fight. The action of that particular fish felt very strange – an action I'd never experienced before. Before long the reason became dramatically apparent. As I put my landing net in the water – the fish took off!!! It was a little grebe – a dabchick – and in no time at all I felt as though I was flying a kite! I eventually reeled it in – as you would with your average flying-fish! Fortunately there was no damage done. The hook had bedded itself into its bill just beneath the tongue and was relatively easy to remove. I placed it carefully back into the water and it skittered off with something of a quizzical look on its face – a bit like mine really! Within a few minutes it was fishing again, popping up and down in the river as if nothing had happened – thank God for that! That was number two of three – not quite as planned, but interesting nevertheless. I re-baited, re-cast and awaited results. The float didn't sail away this time; it just slowly sunk a fraction of an inch or two, and then held position. I struck, for the third time, and although I felt additional weight on my line there was no real struggle! What could this be, I thought – the plug? It was a crayfish. Have you ever handled one of the little brutes? It was like a frigging homicidal telephone receiver! Snicker-snacker! Snicker-snacker! Snicker-snacker! I was very concerned about my very sensitive hominoid digits – it could have rent metal with those ravenous claws; it was horrendous! "You just have to be bloody different, don't you?" said Colin, caustically, "everyone else is happy to catch fish but you've got to go one better haven't you – a dabchick and a frigging crayfish; you pratt!" What could I say – I was *in flagrante delicto* – so to speak! I'd been rumbled; well and truly rumbled!

Somebody else I went fishing with on the odd occasion – odd being the apposite word – was a man named Ian. Now this man could fish – I'm telling you. He'd even been on the front page of the Angling Times with a 30lb carp! I was in awe of his exceptional skills – I really was. He'd think nothing of stripping off and diving into the pondweed to clear a swim for a bit of tench fishing! He was awesome. A lot off his fishing was done very simply indeed – touch ledgering. He'd use as little weight as possible, perhaps a swan shot or two – and then just sit there for as long as it took; almost motionless. I'd fished that river since I was a young boy but he lifted monsters from the deep that I didn't know existed – he was an angling genius. We went all-night fishing together once at Rushes Lock. He fished the back stream next to the tail of the weir and I fished were it came out near the locks back into the main river. I don't know if you've ever noticed just how dark the darkness can be at 3am in the morning – even on a moonlit night! We were fishing a good hundred yards away from each other, so silence and solitariness were the order of the day – or night, if you see what I mean? Behind where I was fishing there was a large, old, gnarled hawthorn hedge. In the silence – the deathly silence – I could apprehend rustling, snorting, and very disturbing scratchy sounds. I daren't look round – I hadn't bought enough toilet paper with me! The noises got louder and louder and the snorting became very demoniacal indeed! I was shitting myself! All of a sudden there was an explosion of leaves and the heart-stopping pound and scuff of diabolical hooves! It's the frigging Devil – I thought; somewhat irrationally. It wasn't of course, it was a frigging bullock, and as far as I'm concerned that was bad enough. A contretemps with a bovine in the moonlit early hours is not my idea of a picnic – so I put a considerable amount of distance between us – POST HASTE!!! When the bullock and his burger-eyed associates finished padding about and drinking in my swim and moved off to pastures new, I gingerly returned to carry on where I'd left off before being so rudely interrupted! I settled back, regained what little composure I could muster, and started to fish. A hare as bold as – well, a hare I suppose – sidled up next to me, sat on his haunches and stared out across the river. I think hares are associated with the Devil – aren't they? Jesus Christ, what a frigging night! It sat there stock still in the moonlight like something cast in silver – frightening, but magnificent. I soon got used to it and was in fact growing quite fond of the little creature. But unlike the hare I couldn't keep still forever – there was work to be done. I lifted my rod to re-cast and it vanished as if into thin air – like any respectable familiar would, I imagine! I thought that I'd had more than enough scares for one night but then something else occurred that had me right back on the edge of my trembling tackle box! In the distance, across the moon-misted pastures, coloured lights began to flash on and off – strange I thought, very strange – not another 'Close Encounter of the Third Kind' I hoped, pusillanimously. What was it? Red and green and white, moving slowly and erratically across the mist shrouded landscape? I'll tell you – Exlax was the last thing I needed!!! As it got nearer, weird, unearthly sounds started to emanate form the futuristic contraption. As it moved closer and closer, carving its way through the mist and my quivering subconscious, I moved off into the hawthorn. Bollocks to the bullocks and their scuffing devilish hooves – when needs must – as they say!!! Gradually all was revealed. It turned out to be nothing other that a charter barge from Paper Mills Lock carrying its cargo of late-night, drunken, disco-revelling aliens! What seemed to me like unaccountable erratic motion and momentum was no more than an illusion. It was just following the natural meanders of the river – nothing more, nothing less; that was all there was to it: so much for space travel – so much for night fishing! I'd just settled back and started 'fishing' again when Ian shouted across to me. "Bring the landing net Merv," he demanded, "I'm into something big!" Like all good boy scouts I rushed immediately into action. I tip-toed across the lock gates like a ballerina on speed, fell into a clump of nettles, cursed – painfully – leapt through the bushes like an antelope, and finally dipped my net in the water to receive the waiting fish. It was a one-eyed roach, well over three pounds! What it would have weighed had it not been optically challenged is hard to estimate – the weight of fish's eyeballs is not something that I'm very familiar with!!! Running the gauntlet of the lock gates, the nettles and the soul shivering darkness, happened another three times that night. Twice to land massive bronze bream weighing over eight pounds a piece, and once to help Ian struggle with an eel that was literally as thick as my arms and must have been 5ft long – HONESTLY!!! It could have been a record for all I know! I told you that Ian was an awesome fisherman – he really was; awesome!

Close to Hoe Mill there was a back stream – overhung by willows and alders and almost impenetrable because of the surrounding nettles – that flowed into the mill pool itself. It was there that Ian taught me some of the finer points of chub fishing. Having used his rod-rest like a machete-wielding native in the jungle to flatten a swathe of nettles, he stood back behind a bush with me by his side and waited for the fish to get over the shock of the nettle clearing. Gradually, under an overhanging alder on the far side of the back stream, chub began to appear. And a goodly number of them at that, ranging from about 3 to 5lb's in weight. The excitement was almost palpable. He cut some mild English Cheddar into half inch squares – for some reason, known only to Chub and Ian I presume - anything other than perfect half inch squares would be ignored! He lobbed a couple of chunks of the cheese into the swim and the chub immediately rose up to meet them – gulp, and they were gone! It was simplicity itself, he freelined a square of cheese side hooked to a number six hook and waited for the line to snatch. Crack!!! And it was on! You needed 10lb line in that narrow back stream to stop the fish from finding sanctuary in the alder roots! The initial lunge of a big chub is something to behold – and hold onto! The fish fought well but was soon netted. A 5lb, large-mouthed, rubber-lipped, stonking chub – incredible! Then it was my turn. I followed the procedure to the letter. The line tautened and I struck. Not a five pounder admittedly, but a healthy, hard fighting junior of about 3½ lb – my biggest chub to date – brilliant! The lessons I learnt about stealth, patience and bait and wait tactics have held me in good stead ever since – thanks Ian, thanks a bunch!

Quite often – especially in the summer – Colin and I used to fish at Rushes Lock on our own. And I mean on our own – there was rarely anybody else to share the swims with – it was ideal. Rushes consists of a lock, a loop of sluggish river, thick with lily pads and rushes, a weir, a weir-pool – naturally – and the back stream -where Ian caught the one-eyed roach - that eventually finds its way under the overhanging alders back into the main river on the other side of the lock. More often than not we fished in the sluggish water above the weir. The swims between the rushes and the lily pads were quite deep – up to six feet in places – and you could catch eels, tench, rudd, roach, perch and bream. I know that there were good bream in there because my elder brother told me of a six pounder he caught. All he did was to freeline a large piece of flake onto the lily pads, pull it off slowly and carefully, and then let it fall as naturally as possible through the water. It seems that it worked time and time again and that the six pound bream was the *piece de resistance!* I never caught any bream of those dimensions but I've had many a good mixed bag of fish from those swims – with some perch to die for! Talking of perch, once for a change, I decided to fish from an apron at the edge of the weir. Fishing in the turbulent, white water beneath a weir is not easy. Right by the sill of the weir itself the water seemed to turn back on itself and form some relatively slack water. I tackled up with a perch float, 4lb line, a number 10 hook and a lobworm for bait. I was only fishing shallow – no more than eighteen inches at the most. I felt that the area of slackish water would attract particles of food that had been washed over the weir and that they in turn would attract fish. I wasn't wrong – in no time at all my float dived under and I was into my first perch. It was a perch a chuck for a while – ranging between ½lb and a 1lb. And then it went dead – only to be expected I suppose! I cast around in the quieter water under some trees and started to catch jack pike up to about 3lb in weight – in was great fun. Then I decided to do something that I'd read about but never actually done. I took the worm off, cast out onto the weir itself, and dragged the hook through the silkweed. I then cast out into the weir pool and let the silkweed and my perch float trundle through the fastest and most turbulent water with my bail arm open. To expect a regular bite in those conditions would have been ludicrous. All I did was watch for any unusual movement of the float: unexpected shifts from side to side, a sudden and equally unexpected halt – anything! The first few strikes were not very fruitful, but then – success! I was into something; something good. A fighting fish, and especially one with the flow of a raging weir pool in its favour, is a battle to relish. When I got it to the net it was a roach – a 2½lb roach – ALLELUIA!!! I caught many more of that stamp on more than one occasion from that particular weir pool - and then they were no more. Where they went and why, I couldn't tell you? I'm only grateful that for once in my somewhat 'incomplete dangler's' life, time and place and specimen roach, all decided to come together – MAGIC!!! The tail of the weir flowed into the back stream so much associated with the awesome Ian! There I fished many times and tried to put the lessons I'd learned from my genial, angling genius of a friend into practice. I touch ledgered with a swan shot and bread flake on the gravel between the streamer weed and caught many roach to be proud of; but never an enormous one-eyed monster nor any of the whopping bronze bream that seemed to come so easily to the awesome Ian! I ledgered with worms and a bomb in the tail of the weir and caught plenty of eels; but never an eel as thick as you arm and as long as a hose pipe - not even as thick as your wrist I'm sorry to say! I freelined under the alders with ½ inch perfect squares of cheese and caught my share of glorious, golden scaled, rubber-lipped chub; but never a one over 3lb in weight. Some people have got it – as they say – some people just haven't!!! Ah well, such are the vicissitudes of life – more downs than ups it seems in my particular case. Not to worry, I caught fish, good fish many of them, what more could your average hunter/gatherer ask for? Rushes Lock is now a thing of the past as far as my particular angling career is concerned. Much I'm sure to the chagrin of some of my readers I've eaten both pike and the occasional perch from that idyllic location and very tasty they were too! Not that I'd do it anymore of course – I'm very much your big white hunter turned photographer and conservationist – such is the way of fads and fashions! The main reason I don't fish Rushes anymore is because of the demands of other factions. Canoeists use the weir as a slalom course, deprived children from the inner cities camp and cause havoc as only aspiring junkies and muggers can, and picnic parties play their ear-shattering transistor radios and splash about with their dogs and rug rats in the best swims! I was even once surprised by a scuba diver as he emerged like a demented seal from the water to adjust his goggles as he paddled about in my groundbait!!! Enough is enough, I thought – and that's for sure! It's time for a holiday I think – a fishing holiday, of course! I was beginning to feel the need of some isolation. People are all right – anglers especially. But there's one problem – they're not like me. I'm perfect you see; I can get along with anyone – more especially myself. I'm the only one who understands me – my psycho/spiritual needs, my creative sensibilities, my natural intelligence, my unrivaled genius where angling is concerned, and of course - my humility!!! I asked an old friend and one-time angler whether he had any ideas and without stopping to think he instantaneously said: "The Lion at Thurne!" So there it was, I phoned them up, booked full board for a week, and found the Norfolk waterways well and truly on my not too distant horizons; CRACKING!!!

INTERLUDE

FISH POEMS

DACE

Darter from darkness –
Shifty in shallows with its hoard of silver.

Twister of the flipped coin –
Shining to shimmers in a cache of secrets.

Fly-catcher – grub-filcher:
Shaker of the tight line –
Dragging the dreamer to a crock of gravel.

Maker of magic on the edge of light –
Forging its mettle into gold concentric.

RUDD

Filament of sudden fire –
Flashing from under to a gush of sparks.

Switcher of circuits on the hatch of flies –
Burnished and blazoned into gold explosive.

Star-splayer – sun-floater:
Dasher of thin glass –
Broken to shatters in a glare of glances.

Mimic of moisture under cloudless skies –
Ringing the stillness to a drench of ripples.

Wing-snuffer – shard-snapper:
Habit of splashes in the quiet dusk –
Rousing the river from its calm reflections.

BREAM

Browser in bubbles:
Dumb to the power of its own momentum –
Flanking the silence with a slab that silvers.

Hump-headed into many facets –
Delver in darkness like a thousand mirrors.

Clouder of clear streams – stirrer of weeds:
A deep-down sow of a fish –
Herding and haunting through a swirl of fins.

Breaker of a tense meniscus –
Thudding from fathoms to the thump of water.

Plunger and poker through a gorge of silt –
Grinding the gravid with a throat of teeth.

PERCH

Epitome of slaughter –
Wise through the window of a world unwary.

Adjuster of unknown refractions –
Quick to the quiver with a spine of arrows.

Fear-hunter – scent-taster – flanker of fine cells –
Tuned to the tremor of innate vibrations.

Blender of whispers through a merge of stripes –
Green into greenness like a doom diminished.

Dream-haunter – gloom-glider –
Finned as a symbol of its red intention.

Catcher of small boys – wonder on the voice of men:
King of the currents in the year's submergence –
Boasting its splendour to a court of frost.

EEL

Essence of evil from the far Sargasso –
Spilling its unction into dykes and ditches.

Sheened into slithers under shales of light –
Oozes its cryptic into ponds and rivers.

Elver to adult through a twist of years –
Adding its inches by the wrench of flesh.

Tunnel of dark blood – coil of questions –
Helix of a deep existence.

Wriggle of something in the silts of sleep –
Brim to the margins of our dry defenses

Spinner of concepts like an involution –
Draws the pretences to the spawn of being.

CHAPTER ELEVEN

THE LION AT THURNE

One glorious Saturday morning in late June I set out for Norfolk – loaded to the gunnels with luggage and fishing tackle – on an Eastern National coach which did the regular return trip from Southend to Yarmouth every Saturday in the summer months. After a tedious and anticipatory journey I eventually arrived at Yarmouth Bus Station. After walking round for a while checking out the bus destination boards I came to the unsatisfactory conclusion that the Broadland village of Thurne had been 'cancelled'! I saw an inspector talking to a driver and went across to speak to him. "Excuse me," I said, politely, "could you tell me the time of the next bus to Thurne?" Both of those dozy dumplings immediately broke into bouts of uncontrollable – and to me unnecessary – laughter. "That be next Friday boy," the inspector informed me – a mite too gleefully for his own good, I thought, "they only goes once a week they do." So this was Norfolk; county of Coleman's mustard, Nelson, and swedes! One bus a frigging week!!! Not an auspicious start – no sir! "You could catch the bus to Repps with Bastwick," the inspector said, in a much appreciated conciliatory manner, "they be running every four hours – on a good day, they be! Thurne only be a fuw country miles from there." It was just about twelve noon. "When's the next one," I asked, hopefully. "That be about ten ter four, give or take a quarter hour or so; you've just missed one while we've been a talking." Bumpkin, I thought, Essex man meets Neanderthal man!!! I wandered off disconsolately to the seafront, found my self a café, and loaded up on swedes and dumplings – burrrrrp! Eventually ten to four arrived – give or take a quarter hour or so – and I wended my weary way to Repps with Bastwick. On alighting in the middle of nowhere I made my footsore way to the local general stores and asked where I could get a taxi. "We don't be havin' taxis 'ere," the proprietress informed me, bucolically, " you might be getting one at Potter Heigham, sometimes they takes the price off a car in the garage showroom and uses thaaart." Frig me – where am I for God's sake – the planet Zog!!! And then my faith in Norfolk and its inhabitants was restored. "Where you be going?" a nice old rusticated gentleman asked me, with a look of genuine concern on his ruddy face, "I'll be givin' you a lift if I caaan." "The Lion at Thurne," I replied, adjusting the shoulder straps on my rod hold-all and extricating a foot from a tangled keepnet, "The Lion at Thurne." "I be living there I be," he said, while at the same time offering to help an overloaded pack mule with his domestic and piscatorial burdens, " you be wantin' a ride?" Thank you Mr. Coleman; thank you Admiral Nelson, and most of all thank you, you swede-bashing philanthropist! We drove down a high banked lane – wide enough for a horse and half a cart - and finally, after an elasticated Norfolk mile or three, arrived at the village of Thurne. Was ten hours of tedium, foot slogging, a contretemps with an interplanetary bus inspector, and two hours talking about fodder beet and mangolds to a rustic restaurateur on Yarmouth seafront worth it? Yes it was – every infuriating bit of it! That place was heaven on earth. That place had everything a village should have: an ancient church – with a graveyard full of buried Christmases; how quaint – thatched cottages, and a pub surrounded by giant, sun-blanched, green-shaded, horse chestnut trees – perfect! As if that wasn't enough, to the north there were endless, uninterrupted miles of prime Norfolk farmland interspersed with isolated oaks, and to the south – more importantly – a dyke connected the village with the River Thurne together with its own white, weather-boarded windmill, followed by more uninterrupted miles of marshes, sky, and the whispering – almost hush – of the susurrating reeds – heavenly!

The Lion at Thurne was a large stone building with a large car park, extensive grounds, and a priceless view of the dyke and the river. The pub sign advertised the fact that it still sold Lacons beer – a Norfolk brew long since gone – and that it was open for business. I walked into the main bar – still struggling to cope with my tackle and my veritable trunk-load of unnecessary luggage – and the manager came straight across to me and proceeded to help me with my gear. "You must be Mervyn," he said, in a very friendly and avuncular manner, "we've been expecting you, have you had problems finding us?" Not wishing to break the idyllic spell I'd just created for myself, I answered in the negative! He said that I was very fortunate because as there weren't that many people staying that particular week I could have the large upstairs room overlooking the dyke - all to myself. Things were looking up – the omens were good! After settling in I went down to the restaurant for dinner. There were three courses and three choices of each. I had a prawn cocktail – well what do you expect, after all, I was very much of a pleb in those days - roast Norfolk turkey with all the trimmings, and finished off with a portion of spotted dick and custard that would have sunk a raft of ravenous ducks!!! Fat, juicy steaks were there for the asking and if you wanted pheasant or partridge all you had to do was give two days notice – and it was all in with the price, no less! Breakfast was equally as appetizing: You could have the traditional full English job – that was so enormous you needed spiky books and a grappling hook to finish it – two fried or grilled, large Norfolk kippers and if that wasn't good enough you could order great, thick slices of home cured Norfolk ham and fresh tomatoes, followed by lashing of tea or coffee and all the toast you could eat – burrrrrrrrrp!!! Lunch wasn't forgotten either. If you were going fishing you were supplied with a flask of hot beverage, sandwiches, cheese and fruit. Quality, service, and value for money were faultless. Nights in the bar were virtually endless! I don't know where the manager found time to fit everything in. If you were still drinking at around three of four in the morning he would suggest – ever so politely – that he would have to be cooking the first breakfasts in a couple of hours and if you wanted another drink perhaps you'd care to take it up to your bedroom with you. As I mentioned at the end of the last chapter, aloneness was my prime objective where that particular holiday was concerned. But you've already heard of Linford's Luck haven't you? There was some cockney pratt staying the same week as me who was in danger of taking friendliness to the extreme. Well, I can 'whistle and flute' with the best of them, but this man was really giving me 'the tom tits'! He just wouldn't leave me alone. I tried to avoid him as if he was a river bailiff with weil's disease, but he would not give in – just wouldn't! He tried to pressure me to go fishing with him time and time again and I was just at the point of running out of ludicrous excuses when the manager told me that the geezer in question had hired a small boat for the week!!! Well, all of a sudden I was all pearly kings and queens. I rushed up the 'apples' in a right anticipatory 'two and eight', knocked on his door and broke into immediate and perfect back slang! "I illway ogay ishingfay ithway ouyay," I said, breathlessly, "OMORROWTAY!!!" The very next morning at first-light we were puttering up the dyke in a small two-berth cabin cruiser – with me espousing the virtues of cockneydom thirteen to the dozen. Well, I was an East Ender myself originally, but at least I had the Hampshire connection to be pretentious about – didn't I!!! It was one of those glorious warm, breathless summer dawns. Ducks were dabbling and quacking; herons were stilted in the shallows with their visors down – looking less than chivalrous; especially if you happened to be an eel – and fish were rolling and swirling on the river's surface. The portents were excellent. We motored down to the mouth of the Thurne where it met the River Bure and moored up where the bream were said to be knee deep on the bottom. But alas we never saw a slab that day – or any day come to that. Since that time I've spoken to many locals on the subject and they've all informed me that the only way to be certain of catching bream in the summer months is to fish all night. Hence our diurnal slab-less-ness!!! But it wasn't a complete loss for 'The Incomplete Dangler' and his Charlie Cotton look alike – not by any means. Roach were feeding - and feeding well. I started off fishing fairly close in with a float but the strong flow was making things difficult so I changed to a ledger and fished worms and bread in the middle. The occasional eel was a bit of a nuisance, but tolerable considering the quality of the roach I was catching. By the time the holidaymakers started moving about in their cruisers we already had a goodly catch of roach a-piece – river-smelling, red-finned, soliloquies in silver – incomparable! I fished much of the week with that reject from the Smoke and despite my yearning for isolation actually grew quite fond of him – not in a 'turtle dove' sort of way you understand! Towards the end of the week, Colin, who had been on holiday in Spain – lucky sybaritic bastard – came down to spend a couple of days fishing. There were plenty of spare beds in my room so there was no problem in accommodating him. This meant that we wouldn't be restricted to the vicinity of Thurne because he also had the luxury of a motorcar. Horizons would be broadened and fish would certainly get bigger – 'certainly'? We tried Ludham on the Ant, Acle on the Bure – by the boatyards – the Stracey Arms, Horning Ferry and Wroxham, also on the Bure – not a bream in sight! It's that old diurnal thing again I'm afraid. If we weren't too busy getting pissed every night we'd have probably been out on the bank catching the hump-headed bastards by the hundredweight! Such is the downfall of those who suffer from an addictive temperament. I'm afraid that fishing that week consisted of fish mainly in the roach and eel category. Not that that was a real problem, especially as you already know my partiality where roach are concerned. But when one fishes foreign waters one hopes to catch some foreign fish – doesn't one! Never mind, Colin and I spent a great couple of days together. The food was good, the beer was even better, and some of the roach were beyond superlatives – job done! We enjoyed the place – and the fishing – so much that when we got home we encouraged Morty, another friend of ours, Dave, and the manager of our local, Tony, to book up for a long weekend so that the five of us could all go together later in the year. Something to look forward to – that's all you need – an adventure!

The summer came and went and we found ourselves one Thursday afternoon in October travelling together down the country lanes to Thurne. That weekend was bound to be a corker: five piss artists and a couple of gallons of maggots all sleeping together in the same room and sharing their friendship and their bodily emanations – 'wonderful'! The first problem that we encountered was mathematical – if not sexual. There were five of us, but only three single beds and a double! Morty was too big for a single bed so the delicate decision to be made was who was going to sleep with Morty. Now Morty was a Scotsman – I have no problem with that – you'll hear no red and white St George type jingoisms from me. But he was an exceedingly large, alcohol-soaked, scruffy Scotsman with a nose like the map of mars and underpants to match!!! We drew straws and for once in my unfortunate life Linford's Luck wasn't playing by the rules. It fell to poor diminutive, blue-eyed, cherubic, luckless Dave to share a hammock with the Loch Ness Monster! Having settled the sleeping arrangements – much to my satisfaction and relief I might add – we repaired to the bar. Tony was something of a connoisseur when it came to gin. His favourite tipple was straight Bols. He asked the manager if he had any – and the answer was in the negative. You could actually see his face sour on the spot – incredible! The manager soon put a smile back on his phisog however. Apparently, there was a pub in the vicinity – the Black Horse – whose governor was also an aficionado on rocket fuel and juniper berries. It appears that there is a Dutch gin called 'Aud de Geneva' or something like that – I certainly don't profess to be an expert on the spiritually disgusting subject! Anyway, we boarded the chariot and headed of for the arena. You know what it's like when two Anoraks get together. Gin, gin, gin, and more frigging gin, that's all they bloody well talked about for hours on end. Well, I may not have yet been pissed-up, but I was pissed-off! Listen, I was a lager lout before C A M E R A's holier than though proselytizing made drinking it a punishable offence! The trouble was that Tony had been a member of the SAS where as I had been dishonourably discharged from the boy scouts for crying over a tight toggle and garter rash! There was nothing for it; I would have to carry on biting my tongue and swallowing my pride as well as my lager. As is often the way with alcohol I slowly mellowed and my sense of irritation softened accordingly. "What does it taste like Tony," I asked, in a foolhardy manner, "is it nice?" "NICE!" Tony responded, with all the gusto associated with *bon vivants,* "it's the best gin in the world – taste some." Foolishly I accepted the invitation. It did taste nice – very NICE!!! Whereas the green-bottled paint stripper that I was used to peeled the lining off your throat, this was as smooth as a virgin's tit – delicious! What is it they say about not mixing beer and spirits? I drunk a few more and in no time at all either the bar was doing somersaults or I was! I felt dreadful. I didn't have to leave a deposit on the bottle – but I did anyway. Mostly in the form of carrots and custard! The landlord wasn't best pleased and suggested that we might like to leave his establishment and return from whence we came – 'tactfully', of course! Well, I was light-headed and somewhat bilious for the rest of the weekend. Never again, I said, but then, I've said that before – many times!

I got up early for breakfast on Saturday morning with a hangover that Mann, Paulin and Crossman would have been proud of and thought seriously of the benefits of euthanasia! But fishing I'd come for – and dedicated pissed-up piscator that I was – fishing it would have to be. Breakfast helped: a gallon or two of strong black coffee to dilute the alcohol in my system and invigorate the neural networks in the angling hemisphere of my brain, and enough dry toast to soak up the Arctic Ocean, was enough to put some stiffness back into my legs and to soften the blows of the boilermaker's hammers bouncing around in my reverberating cranium! We decided to hire a boat between us. A four-berth would be sufficient, we weren't sleeping on board and there was more than enough room for five to fish in comfort – or so we thought! We puttered along the river looking for a likely mooring place. Finding a large part of the bank lined with sheet piles and topped off with concrete, we crunched into the metal sections – less than delicately as far as my vertiginous head was concerned – and moored up. Despite our previous optimism there was no way all five of us could fish on the same side of the boat. So we took to setting up our separate stalls along the bank. Things were starting to go well – trotting the swim with maggots was doing the trick. Plenty of roach and perch were coming to the net and even the occasional skimmer – bream, no less!!! It couldn't last of course – Linford's Luck, you know! As the morning drew on more and more pleasure craft moored up alongside us. Radios blared, dogs barked, ducks quacked as only overfed ducks no how, and children screamed and cried and hollered and hooted all along the bank behind us! It was intolerable!!! We would have upped anchor if we'd have had one, but as it was we just loosened the mooring ropes and set of in the direction of peace and isolationism. There's a narrow no through waterway that comes off of the Thurne about half way between Thurne village itself and Potter Heigham. It's known, like that black American singing duo as Womack and Womack Water. No, I'm only joking, one Womack will be enough for this desultory tale – I much prefer solo artists anyway. Being as the canal-like stretch of water went nowhere in particular, hardly anybody in particular bothered to navigate its overhung, jungle-like, watery tunnels. Perfect for 'five men on a boat' – or off of it as the case proved to be! Every part of the bank seemed to be privately owned. There were more NO MOORING and TRESPASSERS WILL BE PROSECUTED notices on that cut than there are rules and regulations in the British Navy! We'd had enough. Tony, in the best SAS tradition, said bollocks to the capitalist bastards, "WE"RE STOPPING HERE!!!" I disembarked, hung my coat over the no-trespassing sign, and began to fish. The fishing was really good. Away from the disturbance of the continual boat traffic the roach and perch seemed not only ravenous but were at least twice the size - in general, if not in particular - of those we'd caught earlier. Everyone was having a whale of a time and regularly wetting their landing nets. What was it my mother used to say about God paying debts without money? It couldn't last – could it? Some upper class twit, appareled in the archetypal Barbour jacket and green wellies, came wandering across to us with a twelve bore shotgun loaded and ready to fire!!! "This is private land!" he fulminated, "can't you read the notice?" "What notice," I said, innocently, "I can't see one." "Of course you can't!" he blustered, from the chinless wonder of his toffee-nosed mouth - excuse the mixing of metaphors, I'm getting flustered writing this - "you've hung your damn cost over it!" There was no denying that he had a point and I for one wasn't going to argue with a bucket load of buckshot – even the SAS it seems, know when to make a tactical withdrawal! The rest of the long weekend followed a similar pattern: Fish then disturbance, booze and banter, fish and more disturbances, banter and even more booze! All in all I'd say that it had been successful. We weren't going to make the record books but we'd had plenty of good fish, good food, drink and accommodation, and most of all – each other. That's what it's all about in my book: fish, booze-ups and camaraderie – fantastic!

Colin and I often spent time on the Broads on our own, sleeping in his Ford Escort – cramped, but comfortable enough for boozy, unshaven, dog-tired anglers. One place we used to go to quite often was Stalham on the Ant. Not to fish the river itself, but to walk along the bank past the houseboats until you came to the Dilham Canal. It was a lovely little stretch of tree-lined water coming off of the river just this side of where the navigable part of the River Ant ended. You rarely had a problem with boats and there were good swims – especially at the confluence of the canal and the river itself. A little bit of ground-baiting and some loose feed, little and often over the top, and you were usually in for a good session. There, we did catch bream – nothing big enough for the front pages of the angling press – but good enough for us. There were also plenty of decent roach, rudd and perch to be had – very satisfactory! I've filled my boots more than once from that delectable stretch of heaven on earth and I hope to do so again – sooner rather than later. There was one slight problem with the place though – isn't there always? The first time I fished it, every time I heard a loud retort, even though the sky was blue and cloudless, it started to rain! The canal would burst into bubbles as if it was under sentence from a thunderstorm. You've probably already guessed who the culprits were – yes, that's right – clay-pigeon shooters! Why is it that anglers are not allowed to use small-bore shot when the shooting fraternity can fill the rivers up with as much of it as they like? Justice – the law's an armadillo as far as I'm concerned. Still, we've got to stick together: hunting, shooting and fishing – given a chance the antis would see us all confined to the history books – supercilious, self righteous, rejects from the real world of environmental participation; holier that thou observers and kill-joys, sticking their unwanted noses into the rights and recreations of the rest of us. They should stick to soya milk and pulses and leave the rest of us to sharpen our canines and communicate with our more sensible totem loving ancestors. There you are I'm at it again – God I could crush a lentil!!! We didn't always fish the rivers we also fished the broads themselves. These, I'm reliably informed, were all ex peat workings entirely dug by hand – amazing isn't it! Some of them are not connected to the river system and the ones Colin and I used to fish regularly were: Ormesby, Filby and Rollesby. We sometimes hired boats and sometimes fished from the banks where the main roads crossed the broads themselves. In those days you could hire a boat the night before you wanted to fish and go out at first-light. On one particular September day we arrived just before dawn in the thickest early autumn fog you have ever seen. We rowed out into Ormesby Broad nervously, like smugglers revelling in the obfuscating fortuity of the climate! We dropped our mud anchors somewhere – but where we did not know, tackled up and started to fish. Not a bite – not the hint of the merest nibble for hours on end – it was most disheartening. When the sun got up and finally burnt away the fog – we could see the reason why; SEE, being the operative word. The water was that clear I could swear I could see the yachts in Sydney Harbour!!! In those days it was hopeless. If I'd have had the benefit of years of experience I would have known what to do – but as it was I didn't – neither of us did. With water that clear the only option is to go close in to the reeds, the overhanging bushes and trees, or any marginal cover that you can find. Even then you'd have to fish from a distance and be extremely careful how you cast your weight and line. Needless to say we drew a blank, but the sun shone, the temperature rose, and along with it our spirits. We didn't always draw blanks at Ormesby or Rollesby – not a bit of it! We often fished along the roadside from swims amongst the willows and the alders. The water was very shallow close in to the road and the only way to fish effectively was to ledger. My preferred method was a quiver-tip and an open ended swim feeder. Maggots and bread crumb were more than good enough. Roach, perch, rudd, the occasional small tench or bream, all came along and all were more than welcome. Filby Broad was another place we fished from boats – by a pub called – wonderfully I think – the Eel's Foot Inn; if I remember rightly. That was a lovely broad, a vast expanse of water surrounded by tall trees and birdsong – one of the most natural looking broads I've ever fished. Once again I didn't catch anything that was likely to make the water level drop, but the broad held a good head of small to medium sized roach and they made for a wonderful day's sport. We'll be returning to the Broads later in the story and considerably later in my life, but until then we'll leave the highways and byways of Norfolk: the marsh-lined and tree-sheltered rivers, the churches on the top of small hills overlooking God's own waters, like Ranworth Broad or Belaugh and the Bure, the windmills and the reed-beds, the marsh harriers, the bitterns, the spoonbills and the rare and rarified swallowtail butterflies. For now we'll go back to Essex and to Southend on Sea to make plans for our next fishing expedition. And what an expedition it's going to be. Pack your sea rods, your freshwater tackle and your trout fishing gear. This is to be a journey from one end of the British Isles to the other. Have you the inclination, the adventurous spirit, the stamina even? Sort out your Clement's booms, your goose quills and your flies - dip into your pockets and give us some petrol money – come on, be generous!!!

CHAPTER TWELVE

LANDS END TO JOHN O GROATS

First stop Exmoor on the glorious Somerset and Devon borders. Morty, Colin – another friend of our acquaintance; Macko – and my good self were off on another adventure. After many hours of hot and horrendous driving – Morty, being an ex World War Two bomber pilot with about as much road sense as a heronshaw – we finally arrived on the edge of Exmoor. The first problem to overcome was Porlock Hill – a 1 in 3½ precipice with more sharp bends than your average bed spring!!! Morty – with his festering tongue hanging like a razor strop between his teeth – was the acme of concentration as he fought his way round the impossible bends from one side of the convoluted road to the other. It was terrifying! We got to the top – somehow – having passed the escape routes with their heaps of buffering sand, and stopped to replenish our vehicles steaming water supply from the receptacle provided. Then Morty informed us that he'd absent mindedly forgotten to put his glasses on! We'd just suffered two hundred miles of sheer, unadulterated, vehicular terror, and now he tells us – Frigging buffoon!!! Still, at least, now that he had four eyes to negotiate the roads with instead of two, the rest of the journey across the moors might be a smidgen more pleasurable than the preceding perambulatory nightmare! Exmoor is unbelievably beautiful. It's not your average long, stretched out, flat, endless, purple heathery expanse – although they're interesting as well

– it is far more varied than that – and greener. There are so many dips and undulations and steep-sided wooded valleys that you begin to feel as if you are travelling on one of nature's own primeval roller coasters – it's exhilarating! There are clear, cascading streams, scrub-peppered rocky bluffs, grasses, heather, a riot of wild flowers, and above it all the occasional circling pairs of mewing buzzards looking for hares or anything else that makes a dash for life-protecting cover. Eventually we found our desultory way past Countisbury Foreland – the tallest sea cliffs in England at a thousand feet – and on towards another set of tortuous 1 in 3's that took you down into the wondrous valley of Lynmouth. Lynmouth – and Lynton, which is on the top of the moors at the other side of the valley – are known as little Switzerland – and it's no wonder! The place is absolutely fabulous. The steepest of wooded valleys – a double valley in fact – with two racing, clear, boulder-strewn, water-falling rivers, meeting at a location sensibly – if somewhat predictably – named Watersmeet. After the West and East Lyn rivers join, they widen considerably, become tidal, flow under a bridge and empty themselves into the Bristol Channel. The bridge in question is the only bridge I've ever stood on in the whole of the British Isles and regularly watched dippers walking along the river bed in search of food – indescribable! Way up and out on the top of the moors to the north of Lynton and Lynmouth there was a camping site and that was where we decided to stay for a day of two. I can't tell you what it was like; probably well over 1500ft high and in places overlooking the many wooded valleys with views and fantastic vistas stretching beyond belief to the coast of Wales and the mountains farther to the north – incredible! There was a pub half way down one of the valleys right on the bank of the West Lyn – first thing first – don't you think? After a few mid-summer evening beers – or lagers in my loutish case – we decided to have a look at the river. It was very shallow, fast and turbulent, with lots of white water rushing around the boulders and cascading over sills. But every now and then there were deeper and slower sections that flowed into seductive pools. Once our eyes became accustomed we could see small groups of trout hanging suspended in the current. Tiny trout admittedly – 4 to 8 inches at the most – but interesting nevertheless! We hadn't brought any fly gear with us this time, but we did have our bubble floats and decided to give it a go the very next day. We were up bright and early and on the bank before the tourists arrived. What do you mean? We weren't tourists – we were fishermen, and fly fishermen at that! A different thing altogether!!! I had a light spinning rod with me so I elected to use that. The river was very narrow so I thought that a trace of about 18 inches would be more than sufficient for the job. I know that it goes against the grain – especially for the dry fly aficionados amongst you – but I baited up with a 16 hook and a single maggot! I threw a few in as loose feed – again not exactly a dry fly man's preferred method – and cast the bubble float. I didn't have to wait long; trout and natural bait are almost inseparable. I cleared the pool of its small group of even smaller fish in no time. I put the smallest into another stretch of water and kept the 8 inchers for breakfast. Morty, Macko and Colin had done more or less the same thing, so a more than sumptuous feast was assured. Have you ever had fresh brown trout grilled with butter and seasoned with salt and black pepper first thing on a glorious summer's morning? If you have I needn't say anymore – but if you haven't, it's a must – try it! I even pressed my fish-greasy thumbprints onto the postcards I was writing home in order to impress my homebound and hapless friends and relatives! We thought that we might try a bit of sea fishing off the rocks on the North Devon coast. We drove down into Lynmouth – with eyes closed and hearts pounding as Morty played touch and run with the low stone walls dividing us and our precarious vehicle from the precipitous sides of the river valleys – then on and up the ever-tortuous 45 degree inclines that wound their way through overhanging trees and razor sharp rocks and crevices into the cliff top town of Lynton. From there we drove west until we came to the Valley of the Rocks. It was a very impressive place indeed. The valley floor consisted of a few houses, a pub -hmmmmmm! – a cricket pitch and a small caravan site. Either side, sheer, gargantuan rock formations rose up into the blue, white-clouded, sea-salty sky. One of the rock formations – at the western end of the valley and overlooking the sea – was called castle rock; for obvious reasons – it looked like a castle; what else? That jumble of petrified and petrifying rocks was inhabited by of all things – definitely unexpected in Devon anyway – mountain goats!!! All the aforementioned talk of the precariousness and precipitous nature of our perilous travels is as nothing when compared with the life style of those rock-bounding renegades from the Atlas Mountains! They would make death-defying leaps across abysmal chasms, tip toe – or tip hoof, it you understand me – along ledges no thicker the Olive Oil's corsets, gambol about on plateaus with hundreds of down-hurtling feet between them and splattering oblivion, and do all of that without once putting a foot wrong – or hoof, if you see what I mean! They were natural adaptability personified – or goatified – will I ever get the hang of all this biological terminology? I doubt it somehow!!! Further along that high slung valley the road gradually dipped and descended down to the required rocky coastline. There the personification took on more of a paradisal nature. Ragged and recumbent rocks were lapped by the clear, crystalline waters of the blue-green and sparklingly brilliant Bristol Channel. Beds of kelp in varying shades of brown and emerald rose and fell and undulated in the glassy depths, and fish of equally various sizes and colours swam sinuously in and out of the rocks and seaweed. That particular rocky coast was well known for bass, pollack and wrasse and as usual - though why given our past experiences I'll never know – we were ever hopeful! I decided to go for wrasse on a float – sharp hooks being the order of the day for fish with lips that could prise a limpet of the rocks with ease! Colin and Morty decided to ledger into any of the slacker crevices and inlets. Well, after a few fruitless hours we were all definitely in the need of scuba suits and spear guns – it was hopeless – as it nearly always was; unfortunately! Sea fishing abandoned we opted to make our perilous vehicular way down towards Cornwall. We arrived late at night – very late at night – in a lay-by somewhere near Launceston. In the morning – after brushing my tooth, polishing my glass eye, and coughing up trout bones and tobacco juice – I asked the less than sartorially elegant assembled 'travellers' what was next on the agenda. Colin told me that in his book on 'Pixies and Ponds for Grockles' he'd found a likely water close to where we were at that very moment. Good enough for me, I thought, the angle of the dangle – that's all I was interested in! I can't remember the name of that Cornish lake, but it was the archetypal lake to end all lakes – it was idyllic – a tench fisher's dream come true. Overhanging trees and bushes, reeds and rushes, deeps and shallows, lily pads and a surface as flat and glossy black as the best unruffled velvet! Having read all the relevant material we all chose the obvious method – the lift method. Well, out floats sat in that silky, unsurpassable water for hour after motionless hour – Linford's Luck had struck again; though this time it seemed, everyone else had decided to get in on the act! And then just as the light was fading – it happened. I'm not joking; I saw it with my own float weary eyes! Colin's float lifted up out of the water like a rocket, lay flat on the surface for a split second, and then dove straight under like a cormorant with its arse on fire. It's a good job the bite was spectacular because fish and hook had decided against a permanent union – and that was that; another fishless day – ANOTHER BLANK!!! Not to worry, our confidence was soon to be restored. The next day we drove up to the Bude Canal, bought enough bread to negate the miracle of 'the loaves and fishes' and proceeded to bombard the unfortunate canal with groundbait and wishful thinking. And did we catch fish? You bet we did – hundreds of them! That they were all eight inch rudd – seemingly all cast in the same mould – didn't matter in the slightest. We were all in the need of a confidence boost – and that was just the tonic we needed. We fished right up until we couldn't see our floats any longer and all of us emptied our keepnets more than once – a red-finned and another red letter day at last – fabulous!!! We looked in a guide book for anglers and found a trout stream advertised somewhere close to Oakhampton on the edge of Dartmoor: 'private stretch of river owned by local farmer, camping site available with stand pipe but no other facilities'. That'll do we thought, we've got everything we need in the van apart from a water supply – perfect! The farmer took our money, pointed us in the right direction, and then said, casually. "You don't mind pigs do you?" Well, personally I wasn't sure about the subject, I'd only ever known three, and I'd been fishing with them that very week!!! "No, we don't mind pigs," replied Morty, not only agriculturally but having the audacity to speak on all our behalves, "I was brought up on a farm." Yes, I thought, but they were sheep not wild frigging boars! When we got to the field in question we saw a fairly large group of porkers foraging happily in the pink-skinned, curly-tailed distance – no problem! When we opened the field gate however, snouts and ears were instantly raised and a ravening hoard of porcine reprobates stampeded in our terrified direction. "Don't worry about them," said Morty, confidently, "they're alright, just follow me." The sight of a large, dishevelled Scotsman surrounded by curious, ever-hungry, snorting, persistent pigs as he wandered through the wilderness like Jesus with the Gadarene swine - haunts me to this very day! Macko, being short, wiry and quick on his feet, decided to take a chance and wandered off – gingerly it has to be said - in the direction of the trout stream. It was a very good job that Macko was quick on his feet because before he was half way across the field, the porkers, by now convinced that Morty had no food to give them, came charging across to greet - the by now retreating - Macko! When he finally came through the gate like a roach with a pike on its tail we shut it behind him as quickly as we could. Just in time as it happens! Morty sauntered back across the meadow, barged his way – fearlessly I might add – through the ranks of the incipient chops and crispy bacon, and proceeded to tongue lash the lot of us. "Accch! Yer wee timorous cowering beasties, what the frigging 'ells the matter wi' yee all, they're only pigs fer Christ's sake!" "They might only be pigs to you Rabbie frigging Burns," I enunciated, poetically, "but we're shit scared of the rampaging snorters!" He suggested that we all drove down the bank-side in the van and sat inside the vehicle until they'd lost interest in us completely. This sounded good to me; we put it to the vote, and motored off in the direction of another mouthwateringly fish-full breakfast! Morty was right – at least in part – given time they did get bored – or is it boared – with our presence and wandered of to carry on foraging. That was a delightful little stream: clear, cold, and convoluted. Where we were parked it ran through an open meadow, but further downstream it meandered into a stretch comprising small, sheer cliffs interspersed with overhanging trees and bushes. Feeling braver by now, I got out of the van, set up my trusty bubble float rig, and waded into the shallow water. Just as in the West Lyn there were plenty of small trout to be had – and have them I did. Unfortunately, the pigs also wanted them! They must have heard on the porker's grapevine about 'trout a la Merv' and decided to join me in the river! I'd never fished with pigs before – other than the aforementioned humanoid variety – and it has to be admitted that it was quite an enjoyable experience – they were friendlier than I thought. I really enjoyed scratching the sows behind their ears and they seemed to appreciate the gesture as well. But I wasn't sure about the boar, with a hint of sharp tusks and the biggest pair of bollocks you've ever seen – eyeing me up suspiciously! That herd of tusk-denuded tuskers just wouldn't leave us alone. When we were in the van getting dinner ready they spent so much time scratching their grubby flanks on the bodywork that it looked as though we'd been competing in the muddiest RAC Rally on record! Mind you, I have to admit that I did grow rather fond of them and after that particular porcine cum piscatorial experience bacon never tasted quite the same again!!! My final memory of that particular holiday was travelling back home through the glorious countryside of Devon. We stopped and camped by a river that night – the Torridge I think, although it's that long ago that I might be mistaken. Anyway, the river was low and clear and there was not a fisherman – or woman to be seen! That night the heavens opened with a thunderstorm to end all thunderstorms. Hail and torrential rain rattled and reverberated like blasted buckshot on the metal roof well into the early hours. Lightning flashed continuously and silhouetted the surrounding countryside until we felt that we were like both the negative and positive characters fixed on the photographic plates of a meteorological David Bailey! It was horrendous!!! Dawn was very different – blue, bright and exceedingly beautiful. The river, however, was in full spate. Six hours before there wasn't a fisherman – or woman – to be seen. But now, there were more people on that bank than there are on the platform of Charing Cross Underground Station in the frigging 'rush hour' – it was heaving! Did they know something we didn't? Was it salmon or sea trout – I didn't know then and I don't know even now. We were in a rush to get going before the holiday traffic built up – and apart from that we didn't want to make ourselves look foolish by asking any of the locals what they were fishing for! Such is the way with pride – nowadays I swallow it at least twice a day and would ask anyone almost anything if I thought that it would catch me more fish. Pride my arse – what a total waste of time and emotional energy! Big fish and plenty of 'em, that's what I want. Pride can take its pathetic place with all of the other dumb and deadly sins that stop a person from learning their chosen craft – and in my 'incomplete' case – filling their net with whoppers. Pride, envy, gluttony, anger, sloth, lust – HUMBUG!!! Although a touch of piscatorial covetousness doesn't go a miss – does it?

Our next fishing excursion took us to foreign climes – Scotland! Well, foreign to me and Colin that is; for the sheep farming, fly fishing, booze-soaked Morty it was more of a return of the 'Prodigal Son of the North'. We travelled through the night so as not to see too much of

England less we spoiled the uniqueness of our Highland adventure! At first-light we found ourselves negotiating the roller coaster roads of Northumberland – and it was spectacular. It was greener than all the grass on the Russian Steppes and ever so slightly warmer! The Highlands were our destination so we stopped for a quick fry-up and then carried on hitting the gas pedal – if such a description fits a clapped-out Commer commercial van. Edinburgh passed with King Arthur's Seat, two Forth bridges one for puff-puffs and one for vintage fishermen in a more than vintage automobile – and other sundry Caledonian attractions, and before we knew we were in Perth. That was it; the 'Gateway to the Highlands' – our holiday had begun. I was already used to the Northumbrian and Scottish lowland dialects from my days in the army – yes, me a soldier; it doesn't bear thinking about does it!!! But I was completely taken aback by the Highland brogue – not only could I understand it – a distinct advantage over the lowland variety, but to my shame and dismay it exhibited a form of English accent that was far superior to my own estuarial vernacular! Perth was beautiful: tree-surrounded, architecturally varied, and pleasantly undulating – but it was the mountains we were after so we pushed on until we finally reached the deer-haunted braes and glens – and predictably enough; Braemar! Our transport had been playing up since we left Essex. The battery wasn't charging properly and we seemed to have spent an inordinate amount of time push-starting our rust-redundant excuse for a bloody motor vehicle. We decided to make for Morty's home patch – Aberdeen – so as he could put his local brogue to good effect in one of the many back-street garages. The problem turned out to be nothing more serious than a faulty alternator. He purchased an exchange model, had it fitted, and we were ready and raring to go once again. Fishing, that's what we needed to cheer us up, fishing. Morty suggested the River Don - the Dee being a bit too up-market - and not knowing one Scottish game river from another Colin and I readily agreed to give it a fly-lashing! We went to the local tackle shop to obtain our permits to fish and after the proprietor had issued the necessary documentation he looked us square in the eyes with a sort of Rob Roy aggressiveness about his countenance and said – "and I don't want t' see any of ye Sassenachs using MAGGOTS!!!" Strange, easily offended people the Scots – wouldn't you say? We found our way to the wide, relatively shallow, fast flowing river and set up our fly fishing gear. Morty had a nice 13ft split cane salmon rod whereas Colin and I had rods built of similar material but of only half the length! The result of the differences of approach forced upon us by such a piscatorial disparity soon became apparent. Morty suggested that as far as flies were concerned anything with a touch of red in it should do the trick, so he equipped us all with 'red butchers' – perfect, we were off. Well, no matter how hard we tried; Colin and my rod-whistling self couldn't get anywhere near the centre of the river – and incidentally – the fish! Morty on the other hand was catching that many trout it seemed as though he must have had a contract to supply Billingsgate Market!!! 13ft rod versus 7ft rods – no contest. Standing up to your thighs in cold, fast flowing water can be exhausting; especially if the only thing you're catching is the bushes on the bank behind you! By this time Colin had had enough and proceeded to set up his freshwater tackle. "That cantankerous frigging Jock didn't say anything about using worms – did he?" Mused Colin, mutinously, "well sod him!" He freelined a worm using only a swan shot for casting weight and almost immediately struck into a 3lb trout – lunch is served! Morty mumbled something about philistines – but that didn't stop him tucking in to a portion of our ill-gotten gains – did it – hypocritical sheep-shagging git! It was time to move on. We made our way to Huntley – Morty's old stamping ground. He showed us the school where he used to board in winter when the snow was too deep on the hills to allow him to get back home to the farm, and then we carried on all the Spey-sided, mountainous way to Aviemore. Aviemore is a strange place, like a New Town built in the middle of a SSSI. A bit touristy, with hotels, discos, shopping malls and the likes, and yet surrounded by some of the most impressive scenery in the whole of the British Isles. We loaded up with victuals and then made off for a campsite at the foot of the Cairngorms. The next day we decided to drive up the precipitous, narrow winding road to the ski lifts. None of us had ever been on a ski lift before and it was something we were all looking forward to. I didn't realize just how cold it could get up a mountain – a one degree Fahrenheit drop every 300ft – there's that smart arse again – and we were only wearing summer clothes!!! Although it was August there was still plenty of snow left in the high gullies and the wind was blowing steadily from the east. We boarded the cars in a sort of metal shed, were ejected out into the 'invigorating' mountain air, and made our precarious way up to the 4000ft level. If my bollocks had hit the deck on that sub Arctic afternoon they'd have left two of the most enormous craters that you've ever seen – it was bitter! No sooner had we got to the top and investigated the endless heaps of featureless grey granite, and said a few perfunctory words about the thermal properties of snow, than we made a hasty retreat back to the van, and then downwards – mercifully downwards – to the relatively sub tropical warmth of the valley floor – brrrrrr!!! Where to fish next – that was the question. Morty recommended Dunnet Bay near John o Groats and we bowed to his local and superior knowledge. This necessitated a fairly long journey that saw us travelling through Inverness - next to Loch Ness; Morty's spiritual home and beginning of the Caledonian Canal linking the east coast of Scotland to the west – over the Black Isle and on through Caithness to the very northern extremities of the land itself. Caithness is probably one of the most desolate areas of moorland this side of the moon! It was a flat plateau – as most plateaus usually are I suppose – consisting of nothing more than rocky outcrops, festering peat bogs, purple heather and endless wind and rain – it was bleak – very bleak indeed! I've never been so glad to reach the end of land as when we finally arrived at Dunnet Bay. Despite the rain and the wind, Dunnet Bay was beautiful: a rocky, golden-sanded inlet, surrounded by cliffs and the cries of gulls – idyllic! This is the place we thought – who knows what sort of fish there are to be caught in these spectacular northern waters. Who knows indeed? – Morty certainly didn't - so much for local knowledge!!! All we caught was a particularly virulent form of Caledonian flu – another blank! Still, we could always drive up to John o Groats and say that we'd now been to both geographical extremities of these islands of ours – couldn't we. Lands End and John o Groats turned out to be somewhat interchangeable as far as I was concerned: featureless, desolate and undistinguished – rocks and sea; sea and rocks, gull shit, greyness and incessant wind, more sea and more rocks – underwhelming!!! There was nothing for it; after another night's miasmic, fart-ridden, alcoholic sleep, we would be off to pastures new. "Ullapool," Morty said: a sea loch, a harbour, pubs and folk music, mountain reservoirs and CHAR!!! Ullapool it was then; we decided against viewing Cape Wrath for fear of more sea, rocks, cliffs and gull shit, and travelled south down a single track road – if road is the right word – with passing places until we came to a loch and a ferry and a merciful break from Morty's breakneck - and extremely dangerous – driving! I can't remember the name of that particular loch for the life of me, but I don't think there's another place in the entire universe to match its scenery and the extraordinary atmosphere it engendered. It was surrounded by tall, black, grassless and heather-less mountains, the water was as black, calm and glossy as smoked glass, and the sky was cloudless, ice blue and uncanny. The ferry cut through the glass with its bows and the wake fanned out behind us with all the incongruity of summer snow. Apart from the gentle putt-putt of the engine, the occasional cries from the animate, snow-like flakes of the curving gulls, and the whispering slap of water against the hull – all was silence – a deathly, unimaginable silence. I'd never been anywhere before where the sense of infinity was as tangible as it was on that mysterious loch – it was awe-inspiring; it really was. All spells – it seems – must be broken, and that particular one was no exception. We eventually found our way to Ullapool, and Morty was right, it was a special place – very special. The harbour was lined with quaint, stone-built, west coast houses and hotels; it was surrounded by mountainous terrain on three sides, and the other side followed the gull and gannet-haunted sea lanes to the Inner Hebrides and beyond – indescribable! When we got to the stony beach we discovered it to be knee deep in a pink and amber glutinous substance – very strange! For a minute or two we just couldn't think what it could possibly be. And then we saw them in the deep, clear, waters of the loch – jellyfish! Jellyfish the size of which I'd never seen before and have never seen since. Those colourful, translucent entities were up to 4ft across with tentacles trailing down to about 40ft under the water – they were gigantic!!! Morty had been right in another respect, as that night one of the local waterside pubs was putting on a folk music session. We joined in with the whisky-soaked, sea shanty-ed, revelry until we were shown the bleary-eyed, disorientating door, and made our boozy way up to the top of the towering cliffs for a well earned night's sleep. All night – between the sound of snores and other bodily emanations – all you could hear was the bleating of innumerable sheep – Morty must have felt right at home! In the morning, when the light gradually dawned, we saw before us a view of staggering proportions. Hundreds of feet below us creeping slowly out of the loch was the ferry heading for Stornoway on the Isle of Lewis. It seemed so small and so far beneath the circling gulls, gannets, guillemots, razorbills and puffins, that it could have been a child's toy – it was mind-blowing! Its wake spread out behind it like an inverted vapour trail and sea and sky merged imperceptibly into an indistinguishable, perfect and heart-lifting blueness. There was a heaven after all, and we had been given the keys to the kingdom!!! According to the map there was a large tarn situated in the mountains above us and we decided that it was there that we would try our ever-hopeful, piscatorial luck. The road to the tarn was unmade, precipitous, winding and – as far as Morty's driving was concerned – dangerous! As we travelled upwards the wind started to pick up and by the time we got to the top and the tarn it was blowing a gale. The lake was situated on a bleak and featureless plateau. The waves were already coastal-like in proportion and great feathery lumps of spume were starting to blow across its black, unfathomable, non-reflective surface. We parked the van, tackled up, and settled behind some bank side rocks for shelter. We didn't see a CHAR – or a trout for that matter – Morty had one take on his fly and lost the fish and that was that! What we did have – was wind! More wind than a herd of elephants with uncontrollable diarrhea!!! It was blowing that fiercely that the parked van – on more than one occasion – lifted up onto two wheels! Bollocks to that – sea level was calling us loudly and clearly! That was one of the worst journeys that I've ever experienced. A roller coaster in a force 10 storm without a safety belt would have been a piece of piss in comparison – it was heart-stopping! How we got down to relatively safe ground without tumbling headlong over the scree and being dashed to infinite pieces – I'll never know. But we did – most fortunately, we did. The next stop was to be the Isle of Skye, somewhere we all wanted to go – having heard the song – and somewhere where even the dirk-brandishing, sporran-waggling, bandy-legged, kilt-cavorting Morty, had never been before. Over the sea to Skye – what the hell were they talking about? At the Kyle of Lochalsh you could have reached the island with a well-aimed pebble! Bonny Prince Charlie and Flora McDonald were having us all on – surely? Well, I suppose if you're going to dress up as a woman you've got to do something to deflect all the unwarranted, transsexual attention! There's one thing about the Kyle of Lochalsh in August that I'll never forget – MIDGES!!! There were millions of them; and not your normal, harmless, sweet natured southern variety, but north of the border, sword-swirling, red-headed, ravenous Jocks with teeth! Mind you, they weren't at all partisan it seemed – they attacked Morty with as much relish as they did us Sassenachs. We all looked as though we were suffering from a case of the galloping measles – it was both painful and intolerable. We tried insect repellant wipes, but they seemed to attract them even more! They were even coming in through the vents above the dashboard and reached a depth of about two inches. If that wasn't bad enough, herring and black-backed gulls were stamping interminable two-webbed tattoos on the roof of the van, and looking at us with eyes – and enormous beaks – with the sort of malevolence reserved for those who have the audacity to say anything of a derogatory sexual nature about

Bonny Prince Charlie and his flower and hamburger designated partner in crime!!! There was nothing for it, we'd have to board the ferry, escape the midge-ridden mainland, and make for Portree - and hopefully – sanctuary. Portree was nice in a rocky, salt-watery, picturesque sort of way. It had a harbour, traditional fishing boats, ice creams and postcards, and even an angler or two fishing from the quay. But it wasn't for us, we were hardier than that, we were looking for the wilds – the real wilds! We drove right up to the northwest corner of the island – as far away as we could get from everybody else. It was a wonderful place: a rock-redoubtable coastline, hills, deep valleys and spectacular inland cliffs – we were really in our true element. There were buzzards circling, ravens cronking, and most exciting of all, peregrine falcons. We thought that they were probably young birds. They were rising up higher and ever higher on the thermals, circling, stoop-diving, and practicing airborne exchanges – it was an exhilarating privilege to watch them! We didn't fish on the Isle of Skye but we nevertheless enjoyed ourselves immensely. Was there anywhere else we wanted to visit in Scotland before we thought about fishing once more? Yes, there was, of course, Fort William and the ever-renowned, highest mountain in Great Britain – Ben Nevis. That was the first time I'd ever visited Fort William, but I have been there many times since. What is it about Ben Nevis and fog? I've only ever seen that massive lump of Scottish rock in a photograph. You wouldn't think that something that large could be invisible – would you? But it was – and still is – every time I visit that fog-shrouded coastline with Linford's obfuscating Luck as a companion!!! I've given up trying – I'll stick to the photographs – at least you can't get lost and die of hypothermia looking at a snapshot – at least I don't think you can! We decided to have one last go with rod and line in Scotland before heading back down south. We had a quick look at Loch Lomond, but it seemed far too clear, and thick with weed and Glaswegians – no offence fellows, and please keep your ferocious, cranial kisses to yourselves – thank you so much! We settled for Loch Long and some sea fishing. Loch Long is deep – very deep! I'd read in the angling papers all the stories about cod as big and as fighting fit as dolphins and had been mightily impressed. But this was August of course, and you had about as much chance of catching a cod, as getting a Christmas present from an Aberdeen Angus!!! Still, we'd come to fish and fish we jolly well would – God damn it! I said the loch was deep, but I didn't realize just how deep! I thought that my lead was never going to hit bottom and if I did catch a fish its swim bladder would have distended to about the size of the moon by the time I got it to the surface. No, Scotland and fishing would have to wait for another year; it was time to head back into England and to sample the delights of the Lake District. Scotland is notorious for wet weather – especially on the west coast - but apart from the occasional blow and scuds of cloud and rain, we'd been relatively lucky. The Lake District is also known for the odd drop of the wet stuff – or two – and that particular year it lived well and truly up to its diluvial reputation! We were there for five days and it only stopped raining once. Mind you, that once was worth seeing, it was a once in a lifetime experience. As the clouds parted and the sun shone momentarily, the whole of one mountainside captured the striated bands of the heavenly spectrum – the mountainside had become its own rainbow – it was phenomenal! We fished of course, even in the torrential rain. We caught perch and roach and rudd; pneumonia and piles! The rivers filled up and overflowed, campsites were inundated, and tractors employed in dragging the flooded caravans up onto relatively dry land – it was atrocious – it really was. The high passes were cloud-engulfed, the valleys were mist-shrouded and waterlogged, and our clothes, boots, fishing tackle and minds, were sopping wet beyond the wash of any ocean imaginable. We drove into Ambleside, got pissed while dripping mud and water all over the pub's fixtures and fittings, spent another soggy night in a damp and dilapidated, fart-infested van, and then headed for home – and hopefully – dryness!!! After those particular holidays Morty and Colin drifted off in their own piscatorial directions, our membership of the BDAC lapsed, and I was back in solitary mode as far as angling was concerned. I had no vehicle, little money, and an overdraft - what could I do? Eureka!!! I'd do as all good Archimedeans do when they've got a screw in mind. I'd get a moped, that's what I'd do – get a MOPED!!!

Beachy Head

Thurne Dyke Norfolk - looking towards the 'Lion Inn'

Exmoor days

Paradise for mountain goats -Valley of the Rocks - Lynton Devon

Little Switzerland - Lynmouth Devon

Wrasse country

Piscators out west - left to right - the author, Colin and Morty

Trout stream - Scotland

Still looking for Ben Nevis!!!

The glorious 'Lakes' - Wordsworth country

Upton Dyke - Norfolk

'Treacherous bridge' - Potter Heigham

Roach fishing off Heighham Sound
left to right - Ben, the author and Dan

Derelict 'windmill/pump' - River Bure - Norfolk

The Harveys' 'Mayland' - Thurne Dyke - Norfolk

Another roach on hemp - the author - Jacklett's Farm
Bickenacre - BDAC water

The author - high summer - Ulting - River Chelmer

One more skimmer in the net - the author - Stambridge Fisheries Essex

MOPEDS AND MAGGOTS

CHAPTER THIRTEEN

I bought myself a 50cc, pedal assisted Honda moped – and a wonderful machine it was too. I went for the pedal assisted variety because I could drive it on my full car license. It was going to be bad enough being seen by my peer group driving a moped in full motorcycle gear – crash helmet, gauntlets, the lot – without having the unnecessary addition of L plates to add to the hilarity of the spectacle! I did in fact become known as Barry Sheen to the more insensitive of my 'friends'! The part of Westcliff where I lived was far from thief or vandal proof so I decided for safety's sake to keep the mechanized velocipede in my bedroom. I used to drive it upstairs every night and park it beside my bed. A mixture of petrol fumes and roach slime is obviously not the world's number one aphrodisiac and needless to say my sleeping accommodation was never as cramped as I would have like it to have been! Does anyone know a female Hell's Angel with groundbait under her greasy fingernails? Just a thought!!! I travelled many magnificent miles on that two-wheeled, Japanese contraption and caught many fish as a perambulating consequence. I occasionally visited my old haunts, such as Stanford Warren and Woody's, but usually – more for the sake of buttock relief than anything else – fished closer to home. The first place I motored cum pedalled to, was Rochford Reservoir. Now, 'reservoir' may have something of a clinical ring to it, but that was far from the case. Although situated between the Town Centre and the Southend to Liverpool Street railway line, and over-flown by aircraft from the nearby busy airport, it was in fact, a delightful spot. It was a couple of acres in size and surrounded by trees, shrubs, and well-tended gardens – a veritable oasis. It held a goodly head of fish as well. I don't remember any large carp to speak of – though there may well have been some – but I do remember: bream, perch, roach, rudd and tench. It was mostly fished by young lads and maggots seemed to be their staple. They caught fish and many of them, but they were mostly small with only the occasional goer amongst them. In the centre of the lake there was an island with little wooden houses erected for the resident ducks and geese. Many of the local shop and office workers used to sit by the lake in their lunch hour and feed the aforementioned fowl. I reasoned – uncharacteristically for one as 'incomplete' as myself – that with so much free bread going into the lake it would probably produce far better results than maggots; and I wasn't wrong! Roach, rudd, bream and tench, all came to my net by and by, and many of them were quality fish indeed. If I wanted perch, then there were always worms, and they also invariably caught a better class of fish than the ubiquitous maggots! Also, on the outskirts of Rochford was a lake known as Doggets. I'd fished it as a child and remember the big perch I used to catch – or is it just the enhancement of memory? I don't know! Anyway, I decided to give it another go. It was another of the many ex gravel workings scattered about the river valleys of Essex and slightly larger than the average. I went in late June with tench fishing in mind, but when I got there early on one perfect summer's morning I could see the hen fish being chased by the cocks all through the rush-bordered shallows. Not an auspicious beginning – they were obviously still heavily into spawning! A change of tactics was needed. I remembered the 'big perch' of my childhood and decided to give it a go. As you are all no doubt well aware perch can be caught at all seasons of the year – as was proven by my summer escapades on the River Chelmer – but for me they have always been primarily a winter fish, because that was when I usually caught the most and the biggest of them! Never mind, the tench were off limits, and I was raring to go! First of all I tried maggots. Almost immediately I started catching – small perch admittedly – but it was a good sign. After unhooking – with difficulty, owing to the way they swallow the hook – a goodly number of those diminutive, greedy-gutted predators, I decided to up the feed rate. I thought – erroneously as it happens – that if I feed them enough grub, the sprats would soon be full to the pharyngeals and mummy and daddy would come along for Tiffin! I was wrong of course. There was a small perch-mine down there! Right, I thought, look for a shady spot where the ground was still damp and dig some worms. This I duly did and proceeded to fish with my new-found, wriggling acquisitions. But to no avail alas – small perch it seems are insatiable! I decided that enough was enough and that I would give it up as a bad job and make my way homewards. I don't know about you but I always have to have one last cast – at least! And what happened? I cast, the float cocked, and then immediately sailed away. I struck and the rod curved powerfully. I was into a decent fish at last. Could this be my first 3lb perch - I thought, hopefully – but no, the fight was all wrong for perch. It was a 3lb fish though – A tench! Would you believe it – a TENCH!!! Well, life is stranger than fiction as they say – isn't it? I couldn't leave it at that of course, I continued to fish until dusk and the fishing got better and better. I scoured the hedge bottoms and dug up more worms than your average mole. I put a bigger hook on and a bunch of worms to try and dissuade the smaller perch from taking the bait – it didn't work completely of course – but although I still caught some of the little blighters I also caught a number of very respectable tench – job done!!!

Even closer to home was Southend's number one recreation area apart from the seafront – Priory Park. Priory Park is one of my favourite places in Southend. It houses the remains of a Clunaic monastery – circa 1100 – a 15th Century refractory, and a wonderful little museum of local and wider interest – which also houses one of the best natural history sections of its size I've ever seen. The park is a veritable arboretum. There are trees I know: magnificent oaks, beeches, limes, pines, firs and cedars; but there are also many varieties of ornamentals that I couldn't start to name, and in spring, the almonds and cherries are a pink and white perfection of bloom and birdsong. But the real reason we are visiting Priory Park is because of the monk's old stew ponds – which believe it or not still exist to this very day! Two rectangular ponds about 50yds long and 25yds wide sit side by side under the overhanging trees, connected by a small channel and divided by a long, thin; overgrown and bird populated island. It's a little bit of paradise in the centre of town – prelapsarian! Although relatively shallow with an even depth throughout, it held a large population of roach and rudd – some of them bordering on specimen size. The other attraction was carp – large, log proportioned, mysterious carp. In those days, before commercials and the advances in fishing knowledge and techniques – carp, as I think I've mentioned before – especially large carp – were considered difficult, if not impossible to catch. That didn't stop people trying of course – no way! They threw everything at those carp except the kitchen sink – and thinking about it a direct hit would have probably been the only way to catch one. They were canny those carp. Any floating crust thrown in as a freebie was sucked in immediately, but you put a hook in it – NO CHANCE!!! Nobody had the benefit of bolt rigs, zig rigs or pop-up boilies in those days I'm afraid – it was all down to freelining, floats, arlesey bombs, stealth and hope! I never did see anyone catch one of those monsters of the deep – or the shallows, in this case – but knowing the longevity of carp, they're probably still there licking their freebied-lips, and laughing as toothless, venerable old carp only know how, at the pellet-crazy, danglers of Dynamite baits and desperation on the bank! VIVE LA CYPRINIDS!!! The final lake that my moped and I visited regularly in the area – which was also always my first preference by the way – was in Shoebury Park. It was as near as damn it the perfect lake: blue-green, silvery willows, whispering reeds, rushes and rafts of lily pads –

wonderful! I fished that lake in summer for tench and crucian and in winter for perch and roach – as far as I was concerned it had everything. It also had some big carp in residence and at about that time some of the anglers were beginning to ignore all the legends of impossibility where catching them was concerned and had started to take carp fishing seriously. They'd had Dick Walker to learn from in the 50's and 60's and there were new men in the field that were more than willing to share their knowledge of the species with anyone willing to listen. It may not have been Redmire Pool but it was there that I saw my first really big carp being caught. Mostly doubles up to about 15lb but with the occasional fish weighing in at over 20! But then – as now – I wasn't really a big carp man, and I was quite happy to stick to my chosen quarry. It always took a long time to get the crucian feeding. The first bites were shy and tentative, but if you had the patience and stuck with it – loose feeding little and often – you would eventually be rewarded. Funnily enough I didn't use sweetcorn in those days – nowadays you'll never see me without it! I used to loose feed with maggots and fish over the top with bread flake. I know that crucian have relatively small mouths, but I used to use pieces of flake a good inch or even two inches across! And they took it willingly when they were in the mood – by God they did! I've caught crucian in that lake well over the 2lb mark and although they never fed like a ravenous shoal of roach might it was nothing to catch ten or twenty good fish in a session. Tench and bread were also synonymous in those days – though a big juicy lobworm never went amiss!!! Pinprick bubbles effervescing on the surface of a lake and then travelling along in thin lines between the lily pads and the rushes at dawn on a cloudless summer's day is magical – don't you think? It wasn't all summer fishing in those days – I was much hardier then! I fished Shoebury Park in the frost, the snow, and even when then was ice forming around the edges of the lake – and I loved it. So apparently did the perch. Maggots were as good a bait as any and I could easily fill a keepnet with the stripy beauties on one of those short winter days. Most of them were quite small – around the ½lb mark – but occasionally something bigger would come along to make it all worth while – despite frozen hands and numb feet! Sometimes in the winter I'd use a small spinner and if I was very lucky – which I was on a number of occasions – I'd hook into one over the 2lb mark – brilliant! Roach – always more wary and lying deeper in the winter months - required different tactics. A far more sensitive approach was needed as compared with my perch fishing. You needed to think a bit more about the weather and the water temperature as well. I never really did any good in the coldest weather – and a north, or especially, an east wind, was a death knell to roach fishing on that particular lake. I left roach fishing for those calm and cloudy, windless days that sometimes followed a spell of mild weather. You could catch roach in the wind of course, and following a sou'westerly blow was always a good option – but then as now I personally preferred a certain amount of comfort. Perhaps that's why I'm still partially 'incomplete' where angling's concerned – who knows? Anyway, I did catch roach on my chosen days – and good roach at that. I didn't use wheat in the winter, but

I did still use hemp – and very effectively I might add – as well as elderberries I'd frozen in late summer and early autumn. I didn't catch any 2lb plus fish in that lake but I did catch quite a few well over the 1lb mark and on the right day the 'smaller' fish would feed continually. We're back onto roach again aren't we? God, smell those fingers – glorious!!!

At about that time I was doing most of my drinking in the Cricketers in Westcliff on Sea and it was there that I made a couple of new friends – Andy and Stringer. Andy was a British Railway Policeman, straight as a dye, sex mad, and built like the proverbial brick-built shithouse! Stringer, on the other hand, worked as an oil-rag in the print, was as crooked as a pig's tail, one-time 'father of the chapel', with a penchant for anarchy and perverted thoughts! And as for me, I was a medically discharged, limping reject from the British Army with a yellow streak down my back as wide as the Huang He River, who lived by means of Social Security and as much ponsing as I could manage, and had a penchant for strong lager and masturbation! We made The Three Stooges look like the three most famous of all holy than thou archangels: Raphael, Michael and Gabriel!!! A more incongruous and unlikely trio of angling companions you could never imagine – unless you were pissed or insane, of course – or BOTH!!! Andy had done a certain amount of fishing before – quite a bit in fact. Mostly sea fishing – he actually lived next to the very Camper Road Jetty I mentioned in an earlier chapter. He'd also done a fair amount of coarse fishing and was keen to do some more. Stringer hadn't fished very much at all as far as I'm aware, but was also keen to get in on the act. At the time in question he'd taken a photographic course at Southend College and ended up doing freelance work for some of the local newspapers – in fact the photograph on the front cover of this book is one of his; taken on the very day I'm writing about! I decided to introduce them to the Chelmer. It was one of those glorious early summer days, the hay had just been cut – and smelt as sweet as honeysuckle – the sun was high and the river calm; save for the occasional cat's paw of a scintillating ripple or two, and the water was clear enough to scry for fish and future, salacious, fantasies – a might too clear perhaps? We fished where I fished and camped as a child and teenager, by the wooden footbridge between Hoe Mill and Ricketts Lock. Andy and Stringer elected to fish in the shallower, streamer-weeded glide above the bridge, while I walked further up river to a wide bend, looking for deeper and - hopefully - more coloured water! Things, as it happened, weren't too bad in my chosen swim. There was a slight bloom of algae and plenty of marginal cover in the form of reeds and rushes. I fished with my normal summer choice of baits for the Chelmer – wheat and hemp – and was soon into a run of small fish. After about an hour – having not managed to catch any goers – I changed to maggots. BIG MISTAKE!!! Bootlace eels are a regular feature of summer on the Chelmer/Blackwater Navigation and I soon changed back to wheat and hemp! After a while I tried bread flake and was pleasantly surprised by a small tench – but only once I'm afraid! I then resorted to my old favourite – lobworms – and immediately started to pick up some decent perch. I do love the margins on a river – or even a lake come to that – and when the river's as crystal clear as it was on that particular day any form of cover is essential. Time for a break, I thought, and I went to see how Andy and Stringer were doing. Initially they hadn't been doing too well, they could see large shoals of good roach and dace between the streamer weed, but as we all know to our detriment – If you can see the fish, the chances are that they can see you as well!!! But Andy – being more experienced than Stringer – was up to the challenge. He moved upstream of the fish he was after, stood on the bend – which meant he could cast straight down the middle track – threw in some loose feed, waited until it was close to the required spot, and then cast in and long-trotted down towards the quarry. It worked a treat. In no time at all he was into some good roach and dace and from that point on the pair of them never looked back! Night fishing was out of the question. The pubs closed at 10-30pm in those days and long before the arrival of dusk and twilight our tongues took on a tang that could only be alleviated by alcohol! We packed up – not reluctantly perhaps, but with bitter-sweet, fish-haunted memories nevertheless – and walked through the owl-hooting, swift-screeching copse to our vehicle. Warm, cloudless, summer nights; fish in the bag and a country pub to round things off – what could be more life-affirming? We talked the talk, drank the drink, and waxed lyrical in the classic Bernard o Venables, wet and wistful, Liffey-watered style – it was perfection; it really was! Well, it makes a change from strong lager – doesn't it? May all your days on the river be as fulfilling as that day was for

Andy and Stringer and me; and may all your journeys home be punctuated by good friends, good talk, good drink, and memories of such tremendous fish that you'll never have to tell another tall tale for the rest of your time in paradise – tight lines once again my friends – TIGHT LINES!!!

CHAPTER FOURTEEN

BELAUGH TO BECCLES

I've had many boating cum fishing holidays on the Norfolk Broads over the years, so in order not to repeat myself ad nauseam, I'll just mention two of them. The first must have been about twenty years ago. You remember John Anson – my boat-owning, sea fishing buddy? Well, it was with him and his wife Sarah that I made my first real exploration of the Broads by water. We picked up the four-berth cabin cruiser at Somerleyton on the River Waveney one sunny Saturday in September. It was late in the afternoon so we decided not to travel very far. We found a mooring by the bridge at St Olave's – close to the pub!!! John and I – full of the excitement and anticipation known only to anglers – started fishing straight away. Unfortunately the Waveney at St Olave's is not that far from Breydon Water and the sea at Yarmouth - and as is well recognized by most marine biologists, the sea and salt have a certain affinity! All we caught were eels – dozens of them. I wouldn't have minded if they'd been of a decent size – but alas, they were all of the bootlace variety! Still, a pub meal and a 'few pints' soon compensated for the lack of silvers, and we slept the sleep of the just - well, just about! The morning was to have seen us negotiate the wide, sea-like reaches of Breydon Water where the Waveney and the Yare converge – which was famous for spoonbills and nautical mayhem - and then eventually to join the Bure close by Yarmouth Harbour. But as you might expect, things didn't go according to plan! There's only one navigable channel across Breydon Water and that is marked by large upright timbers, painted to emphasize port and starboard. It seems as though Linford's Luck was being transferred to our cabin cruiser. We were no more than a third of the way to Yarmouth when the engine, puttered, petered, and then gave up the ghost altogether! We managed to drift up against one of the aforementioned timbers and lashed ourselves to it – thankfully! Fortunately – as already mentioned – John was a bit of a whiz where engines were concerned; and equally fortuitous, was the fact that he'd brought his tool box along with him. In no time at all, he had us up and running again and it was Hi! Ho! to Yarmouth and the Northern half of the Norfolk Broads. Why they call them Norfolk Broads when there is so much of them in Suffolk – I couldn't tell you! It must be that 'Silly Suffolk' and 'Norfolk Dumpling' rivalry again! Yarmouth Harbour can be a bit tricky in a flat bottomed Broad's boat. At times there is one hell of a tide-rip and trying to get into the Bure without hitting the concrete sides – or missing the entrance altogether – is a job for someone with a 'master's ticket'! We did eventually make our zig-zagging way into the Bure and set a course for Acle. There is flat, and there is – or are, if you wish to be grammatical - the Bure marshes! Between the sea and Acle there is little to see except a winding tidal river, reeds, windmills, more winding river, and yet more reeds. Having said that, I personally, still find it very beautiful: oystercatchers flit and bleep in a black and white checker-work of erratic flight, herons stalk along the margins like clowns on stilts, moorhens and coots squabble and bicker amongst themselves, and ducks in dragoons fly in formation, stretch out their wings as they put their feet in front of themselves, and then cut swarf from the glittering water. If you're really lucky you might see marsh harriers circling overhead or hear the boom of the increasingly rare bitten. Finally, after passing the Stracey Arms and Stokesby we reached Acle Bridge – and another pub! After dinner in the pub and a 'few more pints' we decided to do a bit of night fishing. How Sarah put up with all that eating, drinking, and almost continuous fishing I'll never know – but put up with it she did; and most graciously I might add – and I am still eternally grateful for her forbearance. At least the eels were bigger at Acle than they were at St Olave's!!! Mind you, we were ledgering with worm, so what do you expect? But never underestimate worms, especially on the Norfolk Broads. The bream love 'em, and so do the roach. Fishing for most of the night you'd have thought that we might have caught a bream or two – but no, not a slab to be seen. We did catch some roach though – and good goer roach at that! In those wide, tidal rivers on the Broads I never bothered with a quiver tip, I just used to watch the rod. Even the roach weren't that shy or finicky, you'd get a couple of knocks and then a slow definite pull. That was enough, you hardly needed to strike at all; they almost hooked themselves. The next day we motored up to Horning for lunch – in one of the pubs!!! Horning is just about as picturesque as you can get: a chain ferry, quaint, 'oldie-worldie' riverside inns, period cottages and houses, overhanging alders and willows, professional eel fishermen and ducks and swans by the feathery river-load. Talking of ducks – one of the eel fishermen told John and me that he loved to see the tourists feeding them because it saved him spending money on fattening them up for Christmas!!! Not exactly a candidate for membership of the RSPB – would you think? Fishing was excellent directly off the quayside at Horning. Fishing between the moorings you could bag yourself a net full of small roach, perch, and skimmers – confidence building if nothing else! We fished Wroxham and Belaugh on the Bure with much the same results – plenty of fish but mostly small. Talking to one of the locals at Belaugh – always a good thing to do – we found to our dismay that summer on the Broads was probably just about the worst time to fish! He told us that as the salt encroachment gets farther inland during autumn and winter and great shoals of fish move out of the Broads proper and become concentrated in the upper reaches of all the Broadland Rivers. Well, that's what we heard from a local; nowadays I read that it's exactly the opposite! The experts tell me that because of the amount of rain in the winter the freshwater moves further downstream towards the sea! Life gets confusing for the 'incomplete' amongst us – doesn't it!!! We needed another plan of approach – obviously. If you walk a short distance from the end of navigation at Cottishall you come to a place known as Horstead Mill. Above the mill pool the river is noted for trout as well as coarse fish. The mill pool itself is said to hold good chub, roach, bream and perch – and that's where we decided to fish. We only had maggots and some bread left and John said that we really needed some worms. Now, John use to be a gamekeeper's apprentice in his youth and what he didn't know about country lore was nobody's business. He walked out into a cattle meadow with a bait box in one hand and two metal rod-rests in the other. He turned over a cowpat, stuck one of the rod-rests deep into the ground and started to tap it vigorously with the other. This he informed me, mimicked the patter of raindrops falling onto the earth, and would encourage the worms to rise to the surface. And they did, one after the other, like red plastic tubes being extruded from an injection-moulding machine – it was magic; a miracle!!! Did we catch any bream at Horstead Mill? No! Any chub? No! Any roach? Yes!!! But even smaller than the one's we'd caught from the boat! Ah well, such is life for the 'incomplete', but the scenery was marvelous though – absolutely marvelous! We felt that we might as well try our luck back down south and spent most of the next day on passage to Suffolk. We eventually arrived at Beccles, moored up, and had our lunch in another pub!!! We got out our map of the Broads and mused over the possibilities. Geldeston Lock, we decided; the end of navigation and yet another pub – perfect! I'd fished the non-navigable river Waveney before when I was a member of the Basildon and District Angling club for a short while. We fished a stretch by a golf course near Bungay and it was fantastic. Everybody caught roach, and not small roach, not even what you'd normally call a goer. Those Waveney roach were monsters - I just couldn't wait. The first thing to negotiate was the bridge up river of Beccles. Bridges on the Broads are not normally a problem for small craft, but extremely low bridges and extremely tidal water can on occasion cause difficulties! We looked at the height of the bridge and then at the height of our boat and thought that it would be better if we left the tide to fall for another half an hour or so. Eventually, judgment satisfied, we decided to give it a go – another BIG MISTAKE!!! We had our rods and reels lined up along the top of the cabin and as luck would have it although the boat could have just about squeezed under the bridge on its own, the extra height conferred by the rods and reels made it impossible! It was a mad girder and head-colliding scramble! I managed to get the equipment off of the roof, but was so giddy owing to the crack I'd received on the cranium; I nearly fell headlong into the drink! But we were through – mercifully, we were through. The trip from there up to Geldeston Lock was a riverine, rusticated idyll. Here it was no longer flat. Stately riverside mansions had steep green, flowery gardens that ended in willows and luxurious boat houses. The river wound that much between the overhanging trees that it was always in danger of turning back on itself. Fish were jumping – a good sign – and the water was perfectly coloured – almost the tincture of jade. As we neared the end of the navigation a fisherman on the bank was in the process of playing a large bream – the portents were good – very good! We moored up by the bridge that took you within staggering distance of the pub and started fishing immediately. It was fantastic – at last, a real session! No bream again, admittedly; but enough good roach, dace, and rubbery mouthed chub, to keep an Angling Times staff writer on overtime for a month – we were baggin' up men – BAGGIN' UP!!! The pub it seems could only be reached by boat, or by a mile of bone-shattering unmade road, and as a consequence of this licensing hours were virtually non-existent. It had a generator to work the beer engines but very little else in the way of power. Lighting was supplied by candles and entertainment by a genial Norfolk gentleman with an accordion. They had a barbeque going outside on the green, with steaks the size of a giant's shoe leather – but no where near as tough! It was heavenly – warm, well fed, inebriated, with more than enough fish to talk about without any need to gild the lily whatsoever – HEAVENLY! There's something funny about late September – I don't know if you've ever noticed? The days can be as warm as toast but in the early hours the temperature can drop like the circular appendages on a barrow-load of brass monkeys! We got back on board at about 3am and I settled down to sleep. After a couple of drunken hours of tossing and turning and flying my dipso-orientated plane every way but upright – I felt that a chunda was in order. Well, I staggered along that bank like a blind man with hemorrhoids. When my stomach finally reached my epiglottis, I convulsed, fell over, and found myself up to my neck in exceptionally hoar-frosted grass and steaming vomit – forgive the indelicacy – PLEASE!!! I made so much noise retching to my boot straps and beyond that all the lights went on in all the boats – very embarrassing! John came out in his underpants – adventurously, considering the weather, I thought - to rescue me from frostbite and burning bile, and my very first trip on the Broads ended with a gathering chorus of "can't you two bastards be quiet? We're trying to get some frigging shuteye 'ere!!!"

As I said earlier I've been boating on the Broads many times since then but would like to move forward about ten or fifteen years to the trip I took with my old school friends – Newmangle; who had his son Justin with him – and Colehole; who had his Alsatian dog Solo for company. We were to pick the boat up at Alan Johnson's boatyard at Acle Bridge. The holiday started off ominously enough. As we got to the north side of the bridge Solo decided to have a look at the river. Well, in truth, he peered over the concrete wall, lost his footing and went for an unexpected swim! He was a very good swimmer – but that didn't help. The distance between the water's surface and the top of the wall was dog proof! I held on to one of Colehole's legs as Newmangle held onto the other – Jerome K Jerome would have been proud of us. We eventually managed to drag the sopping, canine weight out of the drink, and watched as the great, ferocious lump, whimpered like a love-struck whippet – so much for our minder! Then we were given the keys to the boat. "Have you ever been on the broads before?" enquired Mr. Johnson, casually. My two piratical friends immediately took one step backwards. "Have YOU?" the proprietor asked, looking me up and down, disdainfully. "Well, yes I have actually," I replied with all the confidence I could muster, "many times." "You won't need me to show you the ropes then," he concluded, doubtfully. "No, I said," with all the assurance of the damned, "certainly not!" In reality, at that time I'd only been used to pretty small craft, both at sea and on rivers. This thing was a fibreglass monster. It was like a furniture lorry with all-round windows and no wheels! But I'd made my bed and somehow I had to prove myself. How I managed to turn that ludicrous vessel into the right direction considering the wind and the state of the tide – is beyond me. But I did; somehow I did, and we were under way! First stop Thurne – I wanted to show the lads my old stamping ground. Somehow I managed to get the lumbering hulk into the dyke and we moored up for fishing and lunch – in the pub!!! After three steak and ale pies, a few bevies; an orange juice and a tin of Chum for the juniors, we went to the end of the dyke to dangle an angle or two. Once again it was roach – the whole roach, and nothing but the roach – but I enjoyed it; I always do. I wanted to go to Hickling Broad and Horsey Mere – both famous for pike in the good old days – but that meant negotiating Potter Heigham Bridge. That must be the smallest bridge on the Broads – if not anywhere! I'd managed to get under it on previous occasion without 'too much damage' but that was always in two-berth craft – our top-heavy, wind and tide resistant juggernaut, was a different proposition altogether! I used three rolls of toilet paper as I tentatively punched the tide in the direction of nemesis. But I need not have feared. Over the years there had been so many land-lubbering collisions with the bridge that the Broads Authority had decided to provide pilots – and what superb sailors they were. They took you under that disastrous bridge at full speed with barely an inch to spare all round – brilliant! I suppose that that was the only way to do it - the only way to counteract the vicissitudes of wind and tide. We turned off the Thurne just before Martham, travelled through Heigham Sound and then turned again into Meadow Dyke. Meadow Dyke eventually took us on to Horsey Mere and we moored up near the staithe and the windmill. I love that windmill – why I keep saying windmills, when in fact, I believe they should be called wind-pumps - I don't really no! It's often open to the public and I can't count the times I've climbed to the top to look out over the surrounding area. There's something about being just there, in that place, between the sand dunes and the sea and the Broadland waterways – it's exhilarating! Desolate, flat, bleak, with vistas seemingly as endless as infinity – yet somehow exhilarating – I just love it! I walked along the edge of the mere on my own and sat next to a man fishing. He was using a swim feeder and a quiver tip and was consistently catching small to medium sized bream – so this is how you do it I thought – and stored my new-found knowledge for future reference. We motored back along Meadow Dyke and then turned towards Hickling Broad. Either side of the river there were vast areas of reed-lined shallows; our boat was far too large to take the chance of mooring in such places, but other, smaller craft were lined up against the reeds and I could see through my binoculars that they were catching lots of fish – lucky bastards!!! We moored up in the dyke by the Pleasure Boat Inn and I for my sins cooked dinner. I know that pubs have featured rather a lot in this somewhat desultory story and you may be beginning to think that much of what I say is purely and simply the result of delirium tremors – but listen on – there's more to it than that. A summer's evening, swallows and swifts skimming the surface of the water, the gentle lap-lap of the wash against the hulls, a pint or two of lager on the patio and a packet of hedgehog crisps – is that Elysium or isn't it? You tell me! I'd seen how to catch bream and I knew where to go to catch them – Irstead Shoals – the name says it all, doesn't it!!! The next day we loaded up with bait and beer and headed for the River Ant and the mouth of Barton Broad for an all night session – Irstead Shoals, here we come. When we got there it was like Piccadilly Circus! All the best swims had been taken by boat-loads of anglers who would probably never move from their chosen mooring from one week's end to another. We must have been a good hundred yards away from where we wanted to fish – but as they say, beggars and all that! We set up our stalls on the bank, threw in enough ground bait to feed the 'five thousand' and waited for nightfall. We never had a bite all night. In the murky distance torches kept going on and off as slimy, great, slithering slabs, susurrated into their waiting alliterative landing nets – it was infuriating. At dawn, Colehole was wandering along the banks with his dog and his shotgun and I really feared for the safety of those fish-surfeited piscators on the edge of Barton Broad. Time to move south, I thought, before our very own man from the wildwoods lost his marbles completely! It was one of the hottest holidays on the Broads I've ever experienced. Temperatures were well into the eighties most days and once or twice crept over the ninety degree mark. A great, wallowing, fibreglass excuse for a boat is definitely not the place to be in weather like that! But we were in for refreshment – a bit too much refreshment perhaps. As we moved closer and closer to Yarmouth we could see a thin grey line rising above the coast. Yarmouth and sea-fog – are notorious bedfellows. We hit that fog like the Titanic hitting its fateful iceberg – it was bitter! One minute it was all

Bermuda shorts and sun screen and the next it was Anoraks and mittens! The temperature must have dropped forty degrees in five miles – amazing! And yet, by the time we were half way across Breydon Water we were back into the heat-wave and sweating like tax evaders. We motored on up the Yare, past Reedham and its swinging railway bridge, past Cantley and the sugar beet factory, and on up to the Beauchamp Arms. The Yare is a difficult river to fish – deep and strongly tidal. So deep in fact that very large coasters use it to sail up to Norwich, and very incongruous they look too, towering above the marshes and the cattle meadows. I've been reading recently that the Beauchamp Arms is very popular with match anglers and that the long pole is the favourite weapon – I must give it a go sometime. In those days I didn't know one end of a pole from the other, and even if I had, I would probably not have been able to cope with the river's vicious flow and the tidal changes in depth anyway! In those days it was ledger or nothing – and ledger we did. Being used to the slower temperament of the Chelmer in Essex I only used to ledger occasionally, but on those Norfolk rivers I had to accept the slippery slopes of the steepest of learning curves and give it a proper go. They taught me a lot those tidal rivers and I still use some of the methods and tactics I learnt all those years ago in Norfolk – THANK YOU NORFOLK!!! Roach were definitely my forte – or were they the only fish 'The Incomplete Dangler' could catch? I caught roach at the Beauchamp Arms and so did Newmangle and Justin – good roach at that. Colehole on the other hand was never that interested in fishing and spent most of his time getting up to no good with Solo and his shotgun! Very conservational – don't you think? Mind you, the rabbits were very tasty! Before it got too late – when all the best pub-side moorings were taken – we moved back up to Reedham. Reedham waterfront is another one of those many perfect Broadland locations: period buildings, pubs, shops and a riverside green replete with ducks and geese and contented holidaymakers. We managed to get a mooring right in the middle of the village centre – idyllic! We sat on the roof of the boat and fished when the tide was almost at the top and starting to slow down a bit. We didn't catch a thing – not even a bootlace. Slack water came – nothing – not a nibble. Then just after the tide turned and the river started to flow more strongly – bites began to happen. Thank you God and especially your right hand man – St Peter – the patron saint of you know who – don't you? We were catching mostly roach, with a few perch, and I for one was perfectly happy with the situation. And then that old green-eyed monster reared its ugly head. Newmangle – of all myopic, spotty-faced, infuriating people – started to catch bream; and decent bream at that! I tried everything I knew – I even lowered my principles and copied the man hook for hook, line for line and bait for bait – nothing – not even a sucked maggot! But at least we'd seen bream on that particular holiday and that was the main thing – I didn't really begrudge him his piscatorial rewards – HONESTLY!!! On our last morning we thought that we'd wander off past Reedham and give the New Cut a go. The New Cut joined the Yare to the Waveney and made an appreciable difference to journey times. We'd only travelled a few hundred yards when I realized that although my rods and Justin's were still there on the river side of the boat roof, Newmangle's and Colehole's, to landward, had disappeared completely! We turned the craft round and headed back from whence we'd came. There was no sign of the missing tackle. We moored up and wandered purposefully up and down the quayside. And there they were, sitting on the roof of another boat! Colehole, wild man of the woods, ex amateur boxer, and general all round 'NO GOOD BOYO', was never backwards in coming forward. "What are you doing with our frigging rods?" he fulminated, somewhat aggressively, "you thieving BASTARDS!!!" "We didn't take them, honest!" came the stuttered and timorous reply," we found them on the green, and nobody seemed to know who they belonged to – honestly!" A likely story was my immediate summation of their pathetic excuse – but what could you do? We couldn't prove anything so we just took our property and left – indignantly. The New Cut cheered us up no end. It was one of the most unlikely looking fishing spots you've ever seen: high, piled and metal-sheeted banks, concrete aprons, and where we chose to fish - a new concrete bridge as well! And yet that cut furnished us with a goodly supply of roach and bream; yes bream – and even yours truly managed to catch a few! Our last day of the holiday was turning out to be something special – and there was even more to come. We made our way back to Acle and moored by the Bridge Inn just opposite Alan Johnson's boatyard. Newmangle, Justin and Colehole wanted to go for a pub meal and a few pints, but for once in my alcohol-soaked life I didn't fancy it and decided to finish off the trip with a late fishing session.

It was simplicity itself: a match rod, 2lb line, a small running ledger, a number12 hook and a loaf of fresh, crusty bread. I couldn't go wrong my friends – NOT AT ALL!!! I had the best roach fishing session I'd ever had – and I'd had some really good ones. Bites were just a slight twitching of the rod tip. Strike quickly - but gently - as the tip went down and you were in. I had a net full of prime roach with none of them under a pound in weight and two or three hovering on the two pound mark – it was phenomenal! What a way to end a holiday? What a way to remember the glorious Norfolk Broads when winter winds drive the fish to torpidity in the depths of the hook-wary, bite-deficient, seemingly roach-less waters of Essex? We still have a few paragraphs to end with where the Broads are concerned – but this time it will be slightly different. In one of my local hostelries – The Plough, Westcliff, I met up with a married couple – Neil and Clare - who lived in Chalkwell. They had two sons Ben and Dan and used to spend a lot of time holidaying abroad in Minorca. They also had two dogs, two cats and a tank full of tropical fish and asked me if I would mind house-sitting for them when they went away. I didn't mind at all, they left me all the food I needed and also gave me some pocket money. They also went to Norfolk a lot. They had their own camper van, a tent - and more importantly - a boat of their very own on the Broads! After a time we all became firm friends and they asked me if I'd like to join them on some of their Broadland excursions. What could I say – heaven had opened its reed-fringed and watery doors and I was to be one of the chosen people – Alleluia brothers and sisters – ALLEUIA!!!

The Harveys were a two car family – or more to the point, one car and a camper-van! There was not enough room for me to sleep either in the van or the adjoining tent, so they very kindly allowed me to use their second vehicle so as I could sleep on the boat which they moored in Upton Dyke – a couple of miles away from the campsite. The first time we went to Norfolk together I stayed with them for an hour or so as they settled into their campsite and then drove down to Upton Dyke to stow my own gear on the boat. We'd arranged to meet up again at the White Horse in Upton at 8pm. When we got there the pub doors were wide open but there seemed to be no-one about. We sat outside for about a quarter of an hour and were beginning to wonder whether or not the establishment was ever open for business! Then a local came over to us. "What you be sittin' 'ere fer?" he enquired, bucolically, "It be open it be." "But there's nobody in there," I replied, in a confused, yet friendly manner, "it's empty!" "Don't you worry about that boy," he continued, "you just get what yer wants from behind the bar and the gov'ner will take the money when 'e comes down." Well, there was obviously far more honesty to the square Norfolk mile than there was to the Essex equivalent – and that's for sure!!! That was a strange pub – strange indeed. When I said it was empty, well that wasn't quite true. The place was chock-a-block with ornaments and curios. Sitting opposite me there was a ventriloquist's dummy. I don't know about you but I've always had a thing about dolls and ventriloquist's dummies. It's the way they look at one with their weird inanimate faces – creepy! I have to say that that dummy quite put me off my lager.

But there was worse to come. On peering into one of the many cabinets thereabouts I espied the largest collection of penises I'd ever had the misfortune to come across. There were appendages of every shape, size and colour you've ever seen! Plastic ones, wooden ones, metal ones, rubber ones and 'ones' made in any other material you'd care to mention. They were also modelled in various states of arousal or otherwise! Strange people these dumplings – it must be the inbreeding! I know I'm a wanker – but that was ridiculous!!! After a few blurred and uncanny hours confronted by the hushed, malevolent, blink-less stares of red-lipped ventriloquism, and the equally unnerving aspect of a seemingly endless, bleary-eyed parade of phallic similitude, I decided to head back to the dyke – no pun intended!!! It can be very dark in Norfolk you know – BLOODY DARK! It was about three quarters of a mile back to the boat and after you'd left the relative safety of a lane with houses on either side – you were into the pitch black of the riverside marshes. Thoughts of Jack-o-lanterns, will-o'-the-wisps, ghosts with their arses illuminated by St Elmo's fire, or any other ignis fatuus you care to mention, had me on such a nervous edge I could have tip-toed all the way to Bedlam and back before I'd had my third nervous breakdown – it was SPOOKY! I eventually found my way to the boat amidst the hoots of owls, the evil cackling of restless, midnight mallards, and the lambent, silvery glow of the full-faced, sniggering moon – frigging lunatic! I decided against fishing, slipped myself nervously into my sleeping-bag, zipped it up above the over-active contents of my imaginative, weary head and wished the world good night –

ZZZZZZZ!!! The next morning found the world far more amenable to those of us of a nervous disposition. The sun was shining, the birds were singing, and the erstwhile cackling mallards were dabbling contentedly in the gold-dashed, sparkling waters of the dyke – beautiful! The Harvey tribe came down to meet me and decided that it was a perfect day for a jaunt up to Hickling Broad. The boys had never been fishing before and Neil suggested that we stop at Lathams of Potter Heigham on the Thurne and get them both some tackle and bait. This we duly did, and then made our way under the aforementioned treacherous bridge and on to Heigham Sound. This time I was in a boat small enough – a two-berth 'Mayland' - to fish close into the reeds in the shallower bays and inlets that I'd never been able to fish before on any of my boating holidays. As we anchored up close to the bank, mud started churning up from the bottom – my, it was shallow!!! On looking into the water I noticed that there was quite a lot of underwater weed, but in-between its snaggy potential there were plenty of large spaces clear enough to fish. Neil and Clare decided that sun bathing was more their forte than angling and left me and the boys the back of the boat to fish from. And the fishing was good – very good. Roach again admittedly, but I for one have never been averse to bit of roach fishing – no sir! We fished with maggots and although we weren't catching any goers, the general size of the fish was reasonable enough. I changed to a lighter float and line – and perhaps paradoxically – changed my hook from an 18 to a 12 and baited up with flake. I immediately started to catch a better stamp of fish – 12oz to a 1lb. In retrospect I feel that if we'd have had a couple of pints of casters we'd have probably done even better than we did – but I certainly wasn't complaining! After lunch and a couple of hours fishing we decided that it was time to make our way back to Upton. As we made our way back down Heigham Sound Neil sailed in too close to the reeds and as we hit bottom the engine stalled. There wasn't enough water for him to get it going again and we couldn't think of a way to get the boat back out into deeper water! Clare – a long-time sailor and all round Goddess of the sea – said something about the ineptitude of 'land-lubbers', threw the mud anchor over the stern, and drew us out into the middle of the river – simple when you know how – isn't it? The outboard started but momentum was decidedly unachievable! Neil tilted it back so as the propeller was out of the water and the problem became immediately apparent – the shear-pin had been severed! "Not to worry," he said, confidently, "I always keep a spare one in the toolbox." The best laid plans – as they say! Not a shear-pin in sight. What to do – a veritable league of Norfolk's nautical miles between us and the White Horse, and there we sat, motionless and inert! Fortunately for us one of the Broads Authority work boats came up alongside and the skipper asked us if were having problems. We informed him of our position – nothing to do with compass bearings I hasten to add – he lashed our craft to his, and towed us two-abeam all the way back to Potter Heigham – a real Norfolk gentleman, I'd say. Neil and Clare and the boys went off to find provisions and a couple of new shear-pins, and I stayed behind to man the ship – perfect. Out came the rods and in came the eels!

Whatever happened to the roach? Never mind, the weather was glorious and I was on holiday – I don't ask for much! We eventually fixed the boat and made our way back to the mooring. After another night's drinking in Upton's answer to the chamber of horrors – they were staring at me again – Ben asked if he could sleep on the boat with me. Neil and Clare asked me if I would mind and I was more than happy to reply in the affirmative. After all, two people shitting themselves in the pitch black has got to better than one – at least as far as fertilizer is concerned!!! It was an unbelievably starlit night in August – the time of the Perseids. The north eastern sky was lit up, even more than it would have been normally, by a veritable firework display of scintillating meteorites – it was spectacular! We had a cup of tea, talked the giggling talk of children and children at heart when on an adventure, and when Ben finally went to bed I climbed up on the roof to look deep into the universe. With so much artificial lighting in the towns and cities – and even some villages – the night sky hardly impinges on our everyday lives. But in the middle of the Norfolk Broads – it's awe-inspiring! I knew a few of the constellations: Ursa Major, Ursa Minor, Cassiopeia, the Pleiades and a number of others. I could even show you the ecliptic and point out a planet or two. But on nights such as that it was impossible. I'm told that at the latest count they have estimated that there are six billion stars in our galaxy – the Milky Way – and that there are equally, something like six billion galaxies themselves!!! Normally such numbers would be absolutely incomprehensible – but not on that particular August night. There were so much astronomical phenomena on view that the sky was far more white than black and to try and pick out individual features was pointless – it was dazzling!!! I try not to think too much about eternal things – unless it's infinite roach were talking about – because such thoughts tend to leave a somewhat hollow and fearful feeling in the pit of my stomach and an irresolvable mathematical conundrum in my confused and more than somewhat - 'incomplete' mind! But on that night I couldn't help myself – anything was possible – even God!!! Morning came as it usually does and Ben and I started a ritual that was to carry on for a number of years – breakfast at the Acle Bakery; or the Acle B-Acle-ry, as we used to call it. What with a full English breakfast, a boat, good companions and plenty of fishing – who needs dreams and fantasies? Not me sir – NOT ME!!! After about a year Neil and Clare decided to move their mooring and settled on one in a small basin at the end of Thurne Dyke – my old and fondly remembered stamping ground. It was the ideal location: good fishing and sun worshipping at one end of the dyke and good eating and drinking in the 'Lion' at the other – perfection! The Lion did the biggest T-bone steak in the universe and that sort of infinity didn't frighten me at all! From that particular dyke we sailed at various times of the year to all points on the compass that the northern half of the Norfolk Broads had to offer. It was 'Swallows and Amazons' stuff – it really was! I remember one September evening coming back up the Bure from Acle when the fog came down almost as instantaneously as the final curtain does on a spot-lit extravaganza – it was miasmic - dusk, no wind, and the fog on the River Bure – extraordinary. A

251

derelict mill held up its ruined sails in the falling and fog-enshrouded light and looked for all the world like some primeval beast haunting the reed beds and the steaming waters. Other craft passed like ghosts in the night on their way to oblivion and their port and starboard lights glimmered like planets in a grey/black universe. We weren't really concerned; we knew the river well by this time and easily found our way back into the Thurne and down to our mooring in the dyke. Days such as those are indelible – they remain in the mind with the shimmering roach and bream, the indefatigable herons fishing the margins tirelessly, the rare bitterns, the coots and ducks and moorhens, and all the wealth and wonder God so generously provided for those with eyes to see and hearts to open – miraculous!

Having a car at my disposal, I didn't always stay with the family and fish the broads and its connected river systems. Sometimes I travelled further afield on my own with a copy of 'Go Fishing in Norfolk' and tried my piscatorial luck in some of the county's most excellent lakes. Two of them deserve a special mention, but unfortunately I can't remember either of their names! Not to worry, I'm sure you won't mind too much if I just point you in the general direction and fill your head with bait, tackle and tactics – will you? The first was somewhere near Aylsham and was what I suppose you would could a commercial fishery – even in those far of days! It was a two lake complex in a woodland setting adjacent to a farm and had a few caravans and camping facilities. I fished those lakes on many occasions over the years and never once had a blank. One of the lakes was stocked with specimen carp and the other was more suitable for the 'pleasure angler'. Needless to say I usually fished the latter! Roach, rudd, bream and tench, were the main species and I had my fair share of all of them. Even an 'Incomplete Dangler' such as I, was usually assured of a good day's fishing. The lake was of a pretty even depth with a goodly amount of marginal features. Tactics were fairly simple. Float fishing on the bottom a couple of rod lengths out or trying your luck with some of the bigger lumps close-in and shallower. Some of the locals used the feeder and although on average they caught better fish, they were fewer and farther between. Tench up to 3lb, roach and rudd to a 1lb upwards, skimmers and the occasional larger bream, all came to the net at regular intervals – a real confidence booster! The other lakes I fished most often were just to the west of the outskirts of Norwich. To get to them you had to drive down a country lane and cross a bridge over the Wensum – which was also part of the fishery. I couldn't tell you now exactly how many lakes there were in that particular complex, but there were quite a few – and beautiful tree-surrounded lakes as they were too. I never blanked there either but the fishing was more natural and harder and I did have some nearly fishless days. But it was well worth the effort because if the fish did decide to feed, you were in for a BLINDER!!! One warm and partially cloudy summer's day in July saw me arrive on the bank at about 11am. As I was tackling up I threw in some pre-prepared groundbait. Immediately the water started to fizz! I couldn't understand it; it wasn't an active groundbait and I didn't think that there was too much air in it, but fizz it did, and it wouldn't stop fizzing! Then I started to notice bubbles; pin-prick, effervescing bubbles. TENCH!!! I couldn't wait to get my bait in the water. I didn't use sweetcorn much in those days – although as I've said before I never go fishing without it now – my favourite tench baits were bread flake and worms. On that particular day I only had bread, but that didn't matter, I was more than confident with flake. I plumbed to depth carefully, trying not to spook the fish and then set my hook at about four inches over depth. I cast in, and before you could say pelvics and pectorals the float dipped a couple of times and then sailed away at an angle of about 45 degrees – I was in! I had four hard-fighting tench all between about 4 and 5lb in quick succession and then lost one as it powered away leaving me with only a tiny section of its pharyngeal teeth! I cast in again and started to catch rudd and roach. Glorious fish they were too, none of them under a 1lb and a number of them approaching the 2lb mark. I was so busy catching them that I almost forgot about the tench. Then I noticed that there were still plenty of bubbles in my swim. Why had I started catching roach and rudd all of a sudden? Why wasn't I still catching tench? I did find out eventually. When I lost the fish that powered away leaving my only with some of its choppers, my float had moved down about six inches as it flew back through the water! You're never too old to learn – are you? It was too late then though; by the time I'd realized what had happened to the float the tench had stopped feeding and it was about time to pack up anyway. Still, I've never forgotten that valuable lesson and nowadays always check my depth if ever feeding fish stop taking my bait! But who cares anyway? I'd caught a 5lb tench – my best ever; and still is for that matter – and more specimen roach and rudd than you could catch in a fortnight in Paradise – fan-bloody-tastic!!! It's time now to leave the Norfolk Broads – and sadly - fishing altogether for a while. Owing to an accident I had while I was in the army I was in sore need of a hip-replacement operation. This I duly had, but unfortunately after the op I sunk immediately into post-operative depression. As if that wasn't bad enough I then started to have panic attacks which subsequently developed into a full-blown nervous breakdown, finding me hospitalized for a few months. Mental illness plagued me for the next few years and not only did I not feel very much like fishing, even life itself didn't seem worth the effort for much of the time. I'm glad to say that those times have passed and at 58 years of age I'm probably happier now than I've ever been in my life. After a number of years off the scene I returned to fishing again this very season and am enjoying it as much now – if not more - than I did when I was a boy – heaven be praised fellow piscators – HEAVEN BE PRAISED!!!

CHAPTER FIFTEEN

'LAST LINES'

Thirty years on and I've joined the Billericay and District Angling Club once again! A lot has changed in the relatively short time I've been away from the sport. Commercials seem to be the in thing nowadays and carp crunching a way of life for most anglers. Margin poles, pop-ups, bolt rigs, hair rigs, zig rigs, pellets and boilies – the world's gone carp crazy!!! When you open the pages of an angling paper you're confronted with that much copy about carp – and barbel – that you'd think roach and rudd had become extinct! Whatever happened to the 'Pleasure Angler'? I've been sucked in with the rest of them. I've bought myself a second hand 13 metre Abu Garcia, Carp Agenda, pole and I'm out there with my 16 elastic slapping the water and bagging up for all I'm worth! My elder brother Dave got me onto the pole and when I'm not fishing BDAC waters I'm out with him at one of two commercials – Stambridge or Hanningfield. But I have to say, that as much as I've enjoyed the experience of catching mirrors and commons up to about 6 or 7lb on the pole the novelty does start to wear a bit thin after a while. I was born a river man and I suppose I always will be one. I can't really see the point of sitting in a bivvy reading a book waiting for one or two - or even three - rod alarms to start buzzing. Okay, you're thinking, he's never caught a twenty pound carp and consequently doesn't know what the hell he's talking about – and you might well be correct. I would love to catch a twenty pound plus fish and I'm already planning an in-line method feeder approach for next summer! But as much as I love fish – and carp, incidentally – I don't really want to know them all by name!!! I much prefer the all-round approach and especially on natural waters. You don't really get to know the stock personally in most rivers – in fact you never know just what's going to turn up – it's a mystery, a glorious, water-crafted MYSTERY!!! But what with river widening, dredging, abstraction, water pollution and the likes, I not sure what the future holds for our glorious rivers and canals? Gravel pits and commercials may well be where the future lies, and the commercials in particular certainly attract a lot more people to the sport – especially young blood – which is just what we need. Angling is coming increasingly under fire from the 'antis' and there's a lot of talk about whether or not fishermen should support fox hunting. Personally I wouldn't go fox hunting if you paid me to – or shooting for that matter – but I'd support their right to hunt or shoot right up to my last breath! I'm sick to death of holier than thou, self righteous, city folk, looking at the rest of us from down the end of their long wagging, supercilious fingers – enough's enough!!! Before long, if we're not careful, fishing will be about as extinct as the FRIGGING DODO! I don't know about you lot but I'm a participator not just an observer, and I'm not prepared to let a shower of smug, self-satisfied, holy Joes – or Janes – spoil my right to enjoy the countryside in whatever way I feel fit – SO THERE!!! When they've toppled the huntsmen they'll start on the wild fowlers and the rough shooters – and then it will be our turn! Don't let it happen friends, brothers, comrades; forget your bigoted blue-collar past and support the toffs and the landed gentry before the homogenizers turn us all into plastic replicas of our former primeval, hunter/gathering selves – stick a live-bait and a treble up their pathetic, proselytizing arseholes before it's too late! Do it now brothers and sisters – join me in the fight for our piscatorial freedoms – JOIN ME NOW!!!

After that highly audible rant I should like to conclude these annals of fifty years of sea and freshwater fishing on a lighter and far more lyrical note. The BDAC has some really wonderful waters and I've been fishing some of them at least twice a week throughout this summer of 2004 – there's that Americanism again! I've used the waggler and the pole and as I said earlier I'm also planning a feeder and ledgering approach for next season – God willing. I've been fishing for carp on the pole at Armigers near Thaxted and have had much success: thirty to fifty pounds a time of prime carp ranging from 6oz to 5lb. I have fished with pellets, sweetcorn, luncheon meat, paste, bread, maggots, worms and casters, and have thoroughly enjoyed myself. I've fished Shalford Farm Ponds for crucian and have relived my youth with more fish than you could shake a stick at! My very first trip to Field Lake at Mountenessing, saw me net a line-whistling bream of nearly 5lb, another of 3½lb and a 3lb tench! On Long Lake I've had small tench from ½lb to 1½lb until they've been literally coming out of my piscatorial ears! On the same lake I struck into a carp on my match rod with four pound line and a sixteen hook and the beast powered off for a good fifty yards before it came to a halt; I played that monster for at least half an hour without seeing it until the hook inevitably gave way – it then surfaced like a veritable Moby Dick and did a heart-thumping splash and victory roll. Did I mind – did I hell! I enjoyed every nerve-shattering, arm-aching, minute of it – it was brilliant! I've been to Jacklett's Farm Lake in Bickenacre to fish specifically for roach on the pole. Have fished with 2lb line and an eighteen hook and caught 30lb plus of roach -and a goodly number of decent rudd – and have been as pleased as a dipso on a piss-up! It's now September and the carp are beginning to cool down as the roach and perch are hotting up! I'm now looking forward to some winter fishing on the many miles of river managed by the BDAC, including a difficult to fish stretch of the Suffolk Stour – with some bream into double figures on offer! I'm eyeing up the River Pant with big roach and specimen dace in mind; and thinking carefully about the Roding at Aybridge, where I'm told simple ledgering with bread flake on the inside of one of the many bends, produces great, golden flanked, fighting chub, that average more than 3lb a piece! I may yet try some pike fishing at Straights Mill or go for some winter bream at Southminster – who knows? What I do know is that fishing has been a way of life with me for as long as I can remember and although I haven't been sea fishing for a number of years I may yet break out my pier tackle and give East Point another bashing! I may well be the most 'Incomplete Dangler' you've ever heard of; but at least I'm an all-rounder – and I'm proud of the fact. Angling has got to be the most glorious sport on God's earth – and never let the 'ANTIS' tell us otherwise. Walk quietly and carefully down to your swim at first-light on a morning late in June. Look for the tell-tale signs: detritus rising in a cloud from the bottom; lines of tiny bubbles speckling the surface, reeds twitching – what more could you ask for? Throw in your chopped worms and Vitalin – flavoured with ox blood or anything else the boffins in the bait industry have come up with – between the reeds and the lily-pads, and cast in. Sit there as the sun begins to rise - red and distended in the east – listen to the dawn chorus and watch the dark silks of the morning water quiver as your float begins to twitch – are you watching? Strike! My friends, strike! You are not dreaming; the test curve of your rod is taking up the strain as a powerful tench runs and dives furiously! Play it away from the lily-pads – put on some side-strain. The line's whistling – give it some clutch – or back wind. It's tiring my friends; it's tiring. You can see it now, it's coming up in the water – and it's a beauty! You've got it now; it's taken a gulp of air – it's done for! Lift its head and draw it gently across to the waiting net. Be careful, it could make a last dash for freedom – turn the water into a frenzy of thrashing white and crystal spray. No my friends, you've got it in the net, it's ten pounds of red-eyed, olive-green magnificence, and it's yours - all yours. Well done my friends – well done INDEED!!!